How to Create Beautiful
QUILTS

CHARTWELL
BOOKS, INC.

KATHARINE GUERRIER

A QUINTET BOOK

ISBN: 0–7858–0543–5

This book was designed and produced by
Quintet Publishing Limited

Creative Director: Terry Jeavons
Art Director: Ian Hunt
Designer: Annie Moss
Editor: Caroline Beattie
Illustrators: Katherine Guerrier, Danny McBride
Jacket Design: Louise Morley, Nik Morley

Typeset in Great Britain by
Central Southern Typesetters, Eastbourne

Produced in Australia by Griffin Colour

Published by Chartwell Books
A Division of Book Sales, Inc.
P.O. Box 7100
Edison, New Jersey 08818-7100

CONTENTS

Fabrics and Fillings for Patchwork

The renewal of interest in patchwork over the last decade has led to a much greater availability of the pure cotton fabrics, which are ideally suited to it. Look through the small ads of any of the patchwork and sewing magazines and you will find mail order firms offering huge selections of printed and plain-coloured fabrics. By sending for their sample packs you will discover the almost unlimited choice available to the patchworker. Investigate other sources such as remnant boxes in department stores, market-stalls and dressmaking off-cuts. Polycotton sheeting, poplin, fine needlecord and cotton lawn can all be used in patchwork as can the lighter weights of furnishing fabric. Keep your eyes open for suitable fabrics and start a collection – ¼ to ½ yd or metre pieces are often all you need for your first projects. Most of the fabrics available specifically for patchwork are either plain or small prints, but larger prints can often be used to good effect so do not discount them. Silks, velvets and taffetas can give patchwork quilts a rich surface texture, but as they are more difficult to handle it may be advisable to save these for a later project when you have gained some experience. Remember that any fabric with a one-way pile or nap, such as needlecord, corduroy or velvet, will appear to change colour if the direction of a pile is changed.

Think about how your quilt is to be cleaned or laundered – cotton is by far the most practical fabric for a quilt that will be used as a bedcover. Save the more exotic fabrics for decorative projects such as a wall-hanging or door curtain.

Try to use similar weights of fabric together; putting a fine cotton lawn next to corduroy would only lead to puckering and uneven wear. However, lighter fabrics can be made firmer by using a dressmaker's interfacing on the back.

Stretch or knit fabrics are not suitable for patchwork; a fabric that may go out of shape during the making of a quilt could distort the fit and ruin your design.

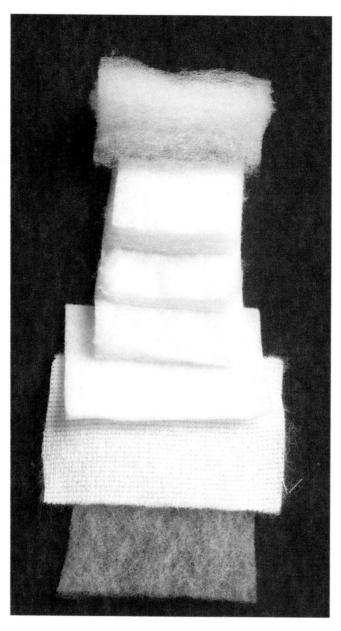

LEFT A selection of different quilt fillers; top to bottom: 1, Different weights of polyester wadding (batting) are available; this is the 4-oz weight; 2, 3, and 4, silk in different weights; 5, Cotton Classic, a low-loft wadding; 6, domette, a woven interlining suitable for wallhangings; 7, needlepunch, a flatter polyester wadding.

Always wash fabrics before using them to shrink and test for dye fastness. If dye leaks out, continue to rinse until the water runs clear. If using old garments, cut away and discard any worn or faded parts.

WADDING OR BATTING

Choice of a quilt filler (the warm interlining between top and backing) can be confusing because there are different types. How you plan to finish the quilt and the purpose for which it is made will affect this choice.

The most economical filler is the polyester wadding (batting), which is available in a variety of weights. For quilting by hand or machine the 2-oz weight is the most practical. Thin enough to stitch through easily, while providing a warm, light interlining for the quilt, it is washable and will not shrink or disintegrate in use even with minimal quilting. The heavier weights (3–6 oz) are suitable for tied quilts and will give a puffy, scrunchy appearance to comforters. Another advantage to the polyester waddings is that they are available in large pieces, big enough for king and queen-size quilts, so there is no need to join pieces for these larger sizes. For smaller projects, wadding (batting) is also available on rolls of different widths. One disadvantage to polyester is that it will blunt scissor-blades and machine needles quite quickly, but this is far outweighed by the advantages.

Needlepunched polyester wadding (batting) is more compact and solid, having been through a flattening process under hundreds of needles, which reduces the thickness while maintaining the weight. This gives a flatter effect suitable for wall-hung quilts.

A cotton filler is the traditional material for quilts – originally teased and carded flat by the quilt-maker, it is now available, prepared for you, by the yard and will give a flatter and more 'antique' look to your quilt, but it is more difficult to work with. It comes off the roll folded with a papery outer skin, and has to be opened out carefully exposing the loose fibres. As cotton will not hang together like polyester it must be closely quilted to keep it in position. The manufacturers recommend that quilts with cotton fillers are dry cleaned; they cannot be pre-shrunk as the filler would disintegrate.

'Cotton Classic' has overcome many of the disadvantages whilst retaining the quality of pure cotton wadding (batting). It is 80 per cent cotton and 20 per cent polyester and has bonded surfaces making it easier to handle. It is also possible to pre-shrink it: to do this put the wadding (batting) into a cotton bag (eg a pillowcase), immerse in hot water and then give it a short spin in the washing machine. Now remove the wadding from the bag, shake it out gently and hang it in a warm place to dry out. Some people like the slightly 'antique' look which occurs when the finished item is washed and the wadding shrinks slightly, puckering the surface fabric.

Pure silk wadding (batting) is now available on the roll, and quilted with silk thread will give your quilt a luxury feel. However, it is expensive and is probably best reserved for small projects or garments.

Terylene or cotton domette (manufactured as warm curtain interlining) is a good filler for wall-hangings and door curtains. It gives a flat surface and a good weight.

ABOVE Useful design tools for patchwork.
~

Watch the manufacturers' advertisements as new products appear regularly, and if in doubt about your choice of quilt filler send to the supplier for samples. Although unseen, the inside layer of the quilt is as important as the two outer layers.

BACKING

Observe people looking at an exhibition of quilts and you will see many of them pick up the corners of the quilt and look at the back. Are they examining the quality of the stitching, or trying to gain an insight into the maker by seeing what has been chosen for the backing? They would be surprised to find in the American Museum, England, a unique double-sided quilt made by two sisters, each side as intricately pieced as the other, but for the underside of a quilt a whole piece of fabric is more usual.

If you are planning to quilt by hand, choose a fairly soft cotton backing so that your needle will go through the three layers easily. Match the weight of the backing to the fabrics used in the quilt top. Sheeting is available in widths up to 108 in (275 cm) but is not recommended for hand-quilting as the weave is too close-textured, making it difficult to stitch through, but it would be suitable for a machine-quilted piece. If you need to join lengths of fabric to make up the size – which should be approximately 4 in (10 cm) larger all round than the quilt size – you will need to cut off the selvedge first because it has a tendency to draw in the edge slightly and cause puckering. Press the seams open.

Remember that a patterned backing fabric will disguise the quilting stitches whereas a plain coloured one will show them off.

Equipment

Essential equipment for patchwork is the same as for dressmaking with one or two additions.

SCISSORS
Keep one pair of sharp scissors only for cutting out fabric, and another pair especially for paper since paper blunts scissors fairly quickly. A pair of fine embroidery scissors is useful for snipping threads and trimming seam allowances.

PINS
The glass-headed variety are easier to see, and they are longer and finer. Keep pins in a pin-cushion rather than a tin as this will make them easier to retrieve when you drop them.

Wedding dress pins are also long and fine, and are suitable for delicate fabrics.

NEEDLES
A variety of sizes is useful. For hand-sewing patches together use sharps number 8 or 9, which are fine and long enough to take three or four stitches at a time. For quilting, short fine needles are best, betweens number 8 or 9 (the higher the number the smaller the needle).

THREAD
You will need a selection of threads for hand and machine sewing. You will find that you add to the colours as you progress, and build up a collection. When sewing patchwork, try to match the thread to the fabric as far as possible. If in doubt, always use a darker thread in preference to a lighter one. Likewise, when sewing a dark patch to a light one use a thread that matches the dark patch.

Quilting thread is thicker than machine thread, and it is better for hand-quilting and sewing.

A THIMBLE
A thimble that fits may be hard to find but is well worth looking for. It will protect your finger and enable you to sew for much longer. Although it may seem uncomfortable to use at first, it is worth persevering if you intend to do a lot of hand-stitching. If you cannot get on with a metal one try the leather type.

WAX
This will prevent knotting and strengthen thread when hand-stitching.

TAPE-MEASURE
An essential item in any workbox, most now have both imperial and metric measurements.

UNPICKER, SEAM RIPPER
More efficient than scissors for unpicking small stitches.

IRON
Patches and seams must be well pressed so either a good steam iron, or a dry iron and mist sprayer, is essential.

SEWING-MACHINE
This will speed up the process of construction for the American method, but all patchwork can be stitched by hand.

FABRIC MARKER
Choose one with which you can get a fine line on the fabric. The fading type of felt-tip marker is a good choice. The line will fade after 24 hours.

SEAM-ALLOWANCE MEASURE
Useful for small measurements.

The seam allowance used in patchwork is ¼ in (6 mm) so a quilter's quarter – a ruler with ¼ in (6 mm) sides all round – is a useful tool both for checking these and making templates.

Cutting out *must* be accurate and takes longer than the actual construction in patchwork, so you may want to invest in a rotary cutter and self-healing board, which will speed up the process. A certain amount of practice will be needed to acquire the skill to use the cutter.

Equipment for Designing

CARTRIDGE PAPER
For papers used in the English method, but used envelopes or paper of a similar weight will do just as well.

SQUARED GRAPH PAPER
For designing and making templates.

ISOMETRIC GRAPH PAPER
Marked out in triangles, this provides an accurate way of making templates for hexagons and diamonds in any size. It is also useful for planning a quilt which uses these shapes.

A BASIC GEOMETRY SET
A set containing compasses, a protractor and a set square.

COLOURED PENCILS AND FELT TIP PENS
It is always useful to try out different colour combinations at the planning and designing stage.

AN ACCURATE RULER
For drawing and measuring templates.

TEMPLATES
A basic set in metal or plastic is a useful starting point, but you will soon want to make your own so that you have more freedom in design. They can be made from good-quality card using a metal ruler and a craft knife or scalpel. It is important to cut them accurately.

MAKING TEMPLATES FOR ENGLISH PATCHWORK

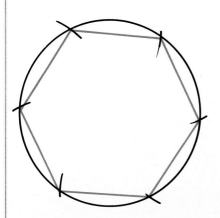

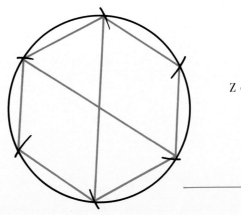

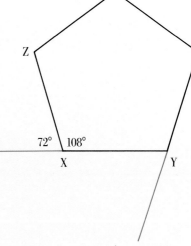

HOW TO DRAW A HEXAGON Set compass to the desired length of hexagon's sides and draw a circle. Using the same radius, place the compass point anywhere on the circle and draw an arc crossing the circle's circumference. Now place the compass point on the crossing point and draw another arc. Continue around the circle until you have 6 crosses. Join these with straight lines to form a hexagon.

DIAMOND Draw a hexagon then connect opposite points to form two diamonds and two equilateral triangles.

PENTAGON Draw a line xy the desired length of the sides. From point x, mark a point z at 108° to the line xy using a protractor. Mark off the correct length on the line xz. Repeat until you have drawn the 5 sides.

Making Templates

The sewing method will determine the type of template you need. For the English method of patchwork, where the pieces of fabric are tacked (basted) over papers and whip-stitched together, the basic template for cutting out the paper pieces should be the size of the finished patch. If a metal or plastic template in the correct size and shape is available then buy one as they are more durable. If you cannot buy the one you need it is possible to make one with a basic geometry set. Any shape or combination of shapes which fit together without leaving a gap (tesselate) can be used in English patchwork. The need for accuracy cannot be stressed enough when making templates. Use a sharp hard pencil (2H) to draw with and cut the template from stiff (though not thick) card using a craft knife and metal ruler.

WINDOW TEMPLATES
These enable you to frame a specific part of the fabric you are using in order to centre a motif. Draw the size and shape of the desired patch on to card, then draw a second outline ¼ in (6 mm) bigger all round. Cut out the centre shape and around the outside line. You can mark the cutting line for the patch around the outside of the template and the stitching line around the inside of the template.

TEMPLATES FOR AMERICAN PATCHWORK
In order to plan a repeat block quilt (a design in which a design unit, or block, is repeated throughout the quilt) you need to be able to draw and cut templates. This will give you the freedom to adapt traditional block designs, and enable you to change the size of a block, add a border or combine features together from more than one quilt.

WINDOW TEMPLATES

patch size

cutting line

Centering a motif using a window template.

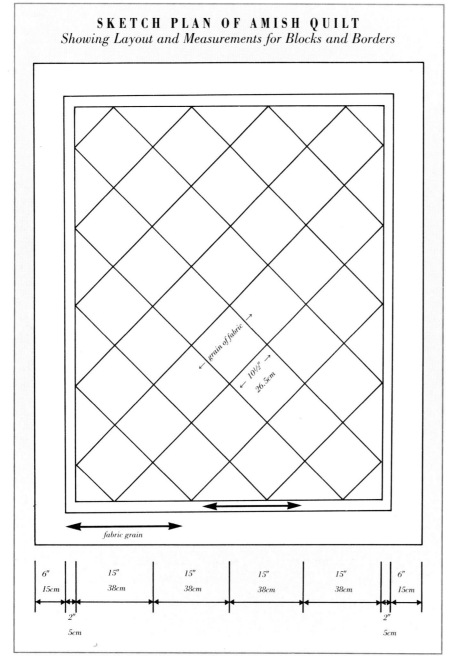

SKETCH PLAN OF AMISH QUILT
Showing Layout and Measurements for Blocks and Borders

grain of fabric

10½"
26.5cm

fabric grain

| 6" | 15" | 15" | 15" | 15" | 6" |
| 15cm | 38cm | 38cm | 38cm | 38cm | 15cm |

2"
5cm

2"
5cm

Next, identify the grid within the patchwork block. In this case it is 3 × 3, known as a nine-patch, so the block must be equally divided into nine 3½ in (9 cm) squares. Draw the block pattern full size onto a piece of squared graph paper and identify the different shapes you will need to make up the pattern. In this case three: a triangle, a square and a rectangle. Cut one of each accurately from your full-size drawing, using either paper scissors or a craft knife, and stick these pieces onto thin card right sides up with stick glue. For hand-stitched American patchwork cut the card carefully, flush with the edges of the graph paper.

For machine stitched American patchwork ¼ in (6 mm) seam allowances must be added before cutting out the templates. Using a quilter's quarter add ¼ in (6 mm) seam allowance to all sides of each shape. You will find that you can butt the quilter's quarter against the shape you have mounted on the base card and draw a fine line around it, giving the correct seam allowance. Cut around this exactly and label each piece with the name and size of the block (Churn Dash 10½ in (26.5 cm) block). Keep them together in an envelope with a small sketch of the block on squared paper as a reference.

Calculating Fabric for Patchwork

To calculate the quantity of fabric you will need for a specific project count how many times each template will be used for any one fabric, adding seam allowances if these are not already part of the templates. Divide the number of times the template width fits across the fabric width into the number of patches needed in that fabric and multiply that by the length of the template. Round this up to the nearest ¼ yd (20 cm). It may help to draw a sketch plan of the fabric noting measurements and drawing the shapes onto it. See the sample sketch plan of the plain fabric needed for the Pinwheel cot quilt. By buying a little extra fabric each time you start a new project you will soon build up a collection to draw from for future scrap quilts.

First decide on the finished size of the quilt, which will affect the size of the blocks you will use. Now draw a sketch plan of the quilt and make a note of the measurements required in each part of it, eg, blocks and borders, in order to fit the design to the final size of the quilt. The technique of drafting patterns and cutting templates is demonstrated here using the Churn Dash block, and it can be used for any geometric block. The quilt in question is 70 in (175 cm) × 85 in (212 cm). To fit the design to this size the blocks must be 15 in (38 cm) from point to point diagonally, the narrow border must be 2 in (5 cm) wide and the broad outer border 6 in (12.5 cm). Any of these measurements could be altered to adjust the size of the quilt. When you have decided on the relative sizes of each part, work out the block size, which in this case would be a 10½ in (26.5 cm) square to give a diagonal measurement of 15 in (38 cm).

MAKING TEMPLATES FOR AMERICAN PATCHWORK

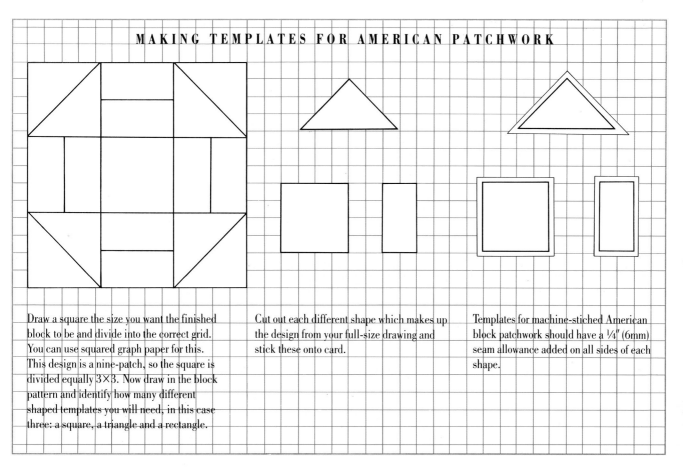

Draw a square the size you want the finished block to be and divide into the correct grid. You can use squared graph paper for this. This design is a nine-patch, so the square is divided equally 3×3. Now draw in the block pattern and identify how many different shaped templates you will need, in this case three: a square, a triangle and a rectangle.

Cut out each different shape which makes up the design from your full-size drawing and stick these onto card.

Templates for machine-stiched American block patchwork should have a ¼″ (6mm) seam allowance added on all sides of each shape.

ESTIMATING FABRIC
Sketch Plan of Plain Fabric Needed for Pin-Wheel Cot Quilt

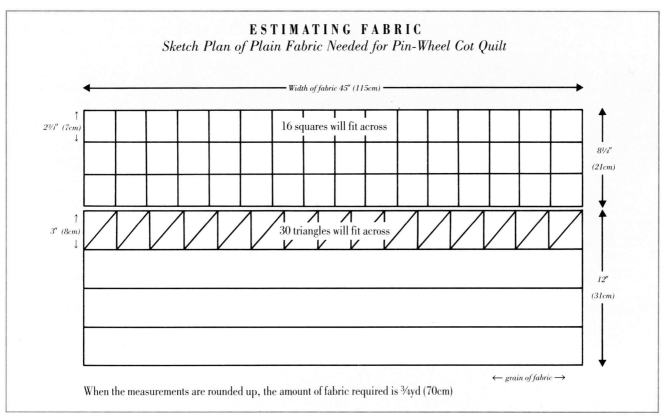

When the measurements are rounded up, the amount of fabric required is ¾yd (70cm)

ENGLISH PATCHWORK

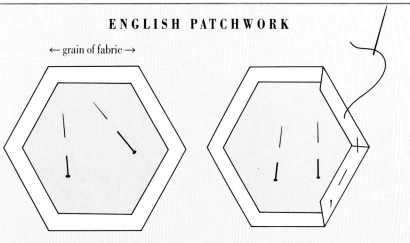

← grain of fabric →

PREPARING THE PATCHES Cut paper shape using template and pin to the wrong side of the fabric. Cut the fabric patch ¼"–⅜" (6mm–9.5mm) bigger than the paper all round.

Fold the fabric over the paper ensuring that the edge of the paper is right into the fold and tack (baste) through all layers. At the corners fold the fabric over and secure with a stitch. Finish with one or two backstitches.

JOINING THE PATCHES Place patches right sides together and oversew neatly. Try not to catch the paper in the stitching. Begin either with a knot concealed in the seam allowance or 2–3 backstitches and fasten off firmly with backstitches.

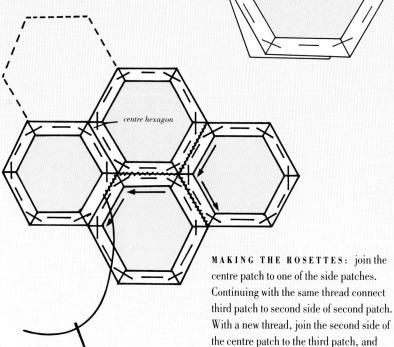

centre hexagon

MAKING THE ROSETTES: join the centre patch to one of the side patches. Continuing with the same thread connect third patch to second side of second patch. With a new thread, join the second side of the centre patch to the third patch, and continue with the same thread to attach third side of third patch to fourth patch. Keep adding hexagons until rosette is complete.

Preparing and Sewing Patches – English Method

Using a template and hard pencil (2H), draw and cut out the shape required from firm paper. Cut each of the papers one at a time; cutting several layers together will distort the shape and lead to problems when fitting patches together. That could throw out your whole quilt. Pin the paper to the wrong side of your fabric and cut out the patch approximately ¼ in (6 mm) larger than the paper all round. The grain of the fabric, that is, the way the woven threads lie, should run the same way throughout a piece of patchwork, so bear this in mind when positioning the paper onto the fabric. If you want to use the fabric in a particular way, eg, stripes going around in a circle, then disregard this rule. Fold the seam allowance over the paper and tack (baste) firmly; finish stitching with one or two back stitches. Use a contrasting thread for this, which makes the later removal of tacking (basting) and papers easier.

Press the patches to form a sharp crease and place them right sides together, lining up the edges to be stitched. Oversew the patches together using matching thread where possible, a darker one in preference to a lighter one if in doubt, and a dark thread when sewing a light patch to a dark one. Begin stitching either with a knot concealed in the seam allowance or with two or three small back stitches, and finish firmly with back stitches. Avoid catching the paper with your stitching. When patches are joined to their neighbours on all sides, the papers can be removed and re-used several times.

When making up hexagon rosettes, begin by attaching the centre hexagon to one of the side hexagons. Take a third hexagon and continue stitching with the same thread round the corner to join the second and third hexagons. With a new piece of thread attach the second side of the centre hexagon to the third patch and continue round the corner to attach the fourth hexagon. Continue in this way until the rosette is complete. Make sure that your stitching goes right into each corner so that there are no gaps.

DIAMOND SHAPES
English Patchwork

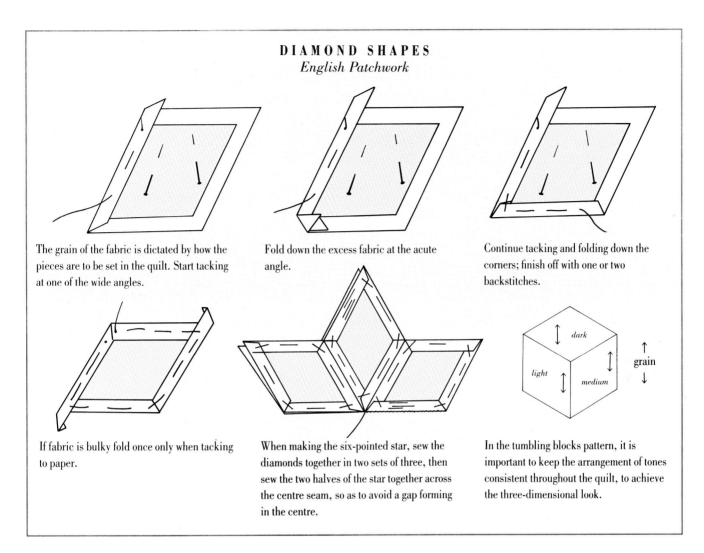

The grain of the fabric is dictated by how the pieces are to be set in the quilt. Start tacking at one of the wide angles.

Fold down the excess fabric at the acute angle.

Continue tacking and folding down the corners; finish off with one or two backstitches.

If fabric is bulky fold once only when tacking to paper.

When making the six-pointed star, sew the diamonds together in two sets of three, then sew the two halves of the star together across the centre seam, so as to avoid a gap forming in the centre.

In the tumbling blocks pattern, it is important to keep the arrangement of tones consistent throughout the quilt, to achieve the three-dimensional look.

DIAMONDS – ENGLISH METHOD
The acute angles on a diamond shape make it a little more difficult to tack (baste) fabric to paper. Pin the paper to the wrong side of the fabric and cut out the patch, allowing ¼ in (6 mm) seam allowance as for hexagons. Begin tacking at one of the oblique (wide) angles. When you reach the acute angle of the diamond, fold the fabric over twice, being careful not to fold the paper into the first fold. The excess fabric in the seam allowance will now be on the wrong side of the patch making it easier to stitch patches together. If you are using bulky fabric, fold the fabric once, leaving a tab at the acute angle. This must be manoeuvred to the back when stitching the patches together.

When making a six-pointed star with diamonds, stitch the diamonds together in two sets of three, then place the two halves of the star together and sew the centre seam right across, thus avoiding having a gap in the centre where all the points meet.

The tumbling blocks pattern, made by sewing three diamonds together, is quite straightforward. Just ensure that the stitching goes right into the corners, so that no gaps occur which would cause a weakness in the patchwork.

If you are making a panel of English patchwork to appliqué onto a background (a Dresden Plate motif for example), press the patchwork with a steam iron or under a damp cloth when you have finished assembling it, before carefully removing the papers. This creates a sharp crease around the outer edge. Tack (baste) down the turnings around the outer edge before positioning the work onto the background, then pin and tack down the motif,

smoothing it flat over the background, and stitch neatly by hand or machine. Lastly, remove all tacking stitches.

FINISHING ENGLISH PATCHWORK
More often than not the shapes used in English patchwork do not give the quilt top straight edges, but there are various ways of solving this problem.

For the first method: when the patchwork is finished, press the edges before carefully removing the papers. Then draw a straight line along the sides of the patchwork where the border or binding is to be attached. Now cut through the patchwork along this line. This makes it possible to attach a straight or mitred border to the patchwork as described in 'Borders' (see below).

Another method is to appliqué the edges of the patchwork to a straight border. To

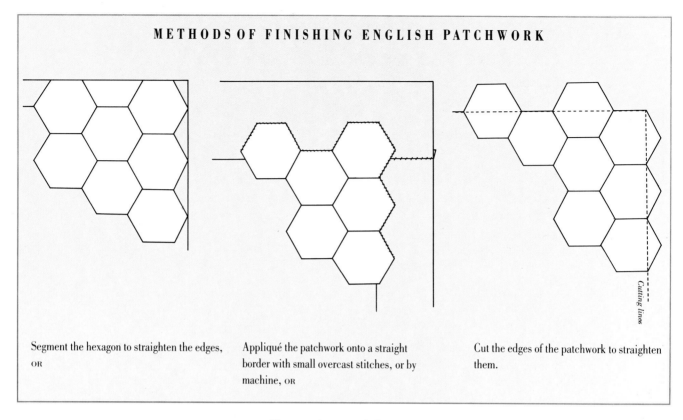

METHODS OF FINISHING ENGLISH PATCHWORK

Segment the hexagon to straighten the edges, OR

Appliqué the patchwork onto a straight border with small overcast stitches, or by machine, OR

Cut the edges of the patchwork to straighten them.

Cutting lines

do this cut two border strips for the shorter sides first. Make them wide enough to form a border on the wrong side of the patchwork as well, and long enough at each end to accommodate the borders for the longer sides which are added later. Turn under the long edge of the side which is to go under the patchwork, by pressing ¼ in (6 mm) of fabric to the wrong side, and then pin and stitch the patchwork to the border by hand or machine. Now cut the borders for the longer sides to the same width, and long enough to reach under the border on the shorter sides. Pin and stitch the patchwork onto the long borders, then slip hem the short borders onto the long borders (refer to the diagram).

Or you can segment the hexagon and cut papers to fit the gaps round the sides. Cover the papers as you would for complete hexagons and fit and stitch these into the gaps thus straightening the sides of the patchwork. When finished like this, the edges of the patchwork are folded under. Press firmly to fix the creases before removing the papers. Now stitch the straight sides to border strips as for the appliqué method.

Preparing and Sewing Patches – American Method

HAND STITCHED

When making up blocks in American patchwork the grain of the fabric should run parallel with the straight sides of the block. Mark a straight line on each template to indicate how you will position it on the fabric. Place the template on the wrong side of your fabric, remembering to turn over any asymmetrical template, for example, a rhomboid, so as not to cut a mirror image patch. Draw around each template with a fabric marker leaving enough space between them to add seam allowances when cutting out. Since the line you have marked is the stitching line, cut out each shape adding a ¼ in (6 mm) all around the marked line. You can either draw the cutting line onto the fabric or measure by eye. When you have cut out all the patches in one block, place them together on a flat surface in the correct positions.

ORDER OF PIECING

The two basic rules are to start with the smaller patches, and stitch in straight lines where possible. For the Churn Dash block, for example, you would start by assembling the triangles and rectangles into squares, join these squares into rows, and finally join the three rows of squares together. However, if you are sewing a block in which it is necessary to stitch into a corner to set in a piece, pin the first two edges to be stitched together (the two that create the corner) and sew up to the seam allowance (not to the edge of the fabric), then sew the third piece to one side of the angle up to the corner, pivot the fabric and continue sewing the second part of the seam.

STITCHING

Place the patches right sides together and pin, with the marked stitching lines matching up. When hand-stitching patches together, use a neat running stitch on the marked sewing lines of each piece. Place the patches to be joined right sides together and match the lines with pins. The stitching should start and end at each seam line (not the edge of the fabric, see diagram) and should always start with a small knot or back stitch and finish firmly with

PIECING ORDER FOR AMERICAN BLOCKS

Arrange the pieces of the block in the correct position.

Assemble each square.

←grain of fabric →

Sew the squares together in rows.

Join the rows to form one block.

PIECING:
Setting a Piece into a Corner

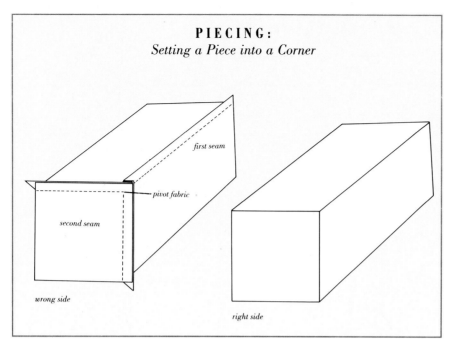

first seam

pivot fabric

second seam

wrong side

right side

HANDSTITCHED AMERICAN PATCHWORK

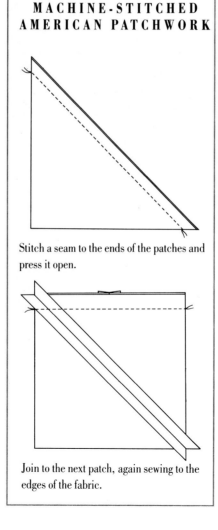

Start and end the seam on the marked stitching line.

Press all seams to one side, the darker side if possible.

MACHINE-STITCHED AMERICAN PATCHWORK

Stitch a seam to the ends of the patches and press it open.

Join to the next patch, again sewing to the edges of the fabric.

a back stitch or two to prevent the seams from coming undone. Waxing will prevent the thread from knotting to some extent. Seam allowances should be pressed to one side, to the darker side of the seam where possible. When quilted this makes stronger seams and prevents the stitches from bulging open.

MACHINE STITCHED

Patches cut with templates made for machine piecing already have the seam allowance added. Piecing order follows the same principles as for hand stitched patchwork – smaller patches into larger ones and straight lines of stitching where possible. Machine-stitched seams are stronger and can be pressed open. Place patches right sides together and guide the raw edge against the presser foot – most sewing-machines will give a ¼ in (6 mm) seam allowance. If yours does not, mark the plate on your machine parallel to the seam line and ¼ in (6 mm) from the needle using a narrow strip of masking tape and use that as a seam guide.

PIECING ANGLED SHAPES

When joining shapes that run at an angle, other than a right angle, eg, diamonds and triangles, align the stitching lines, *not* the cut edges. This makes a straight edge when the patches are opened.

MATCHING POINTS

Some blocks have a point at which four or more fabrics meet. To match these points accurately, push a pin through at the exact spot where the points are to be matched at a right angle to your stitching. Stitch up to the pin, remove carefully and stitch over the point.

Appliqué

Appliqué, from the French word to apply, is the technique of cutting out pieces of material and stitching them to a background. This was a way of extending the life of a garment or bedspread which had become worn in places, or of making expensive pieces of material go further. Various motifs, including flora and fauna were cut and stitched into elaborate de-

PIECING ANGLED SHAPES

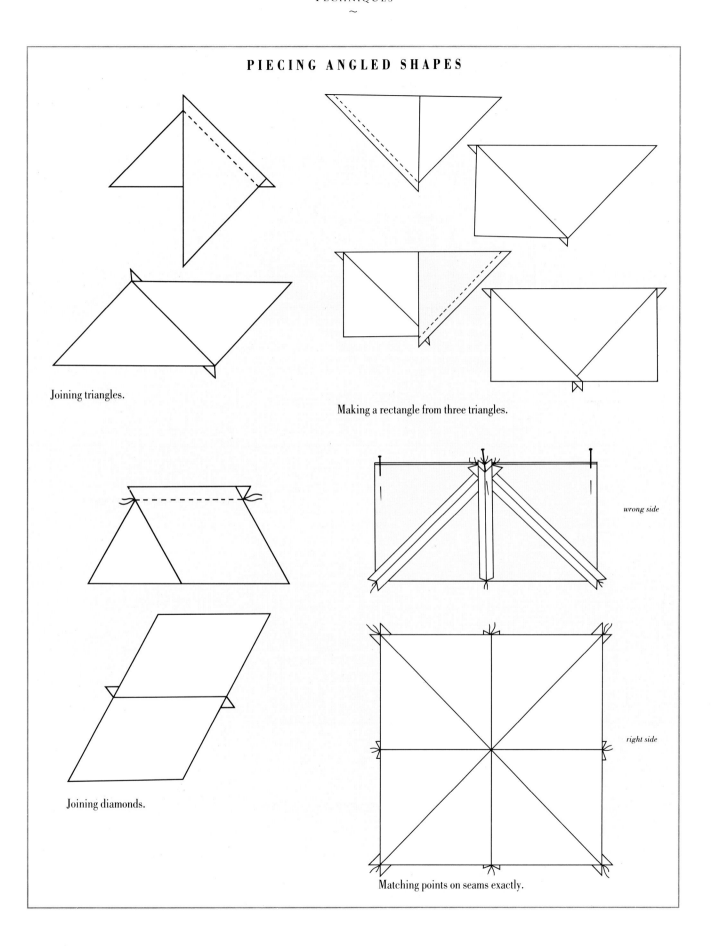

Joining triangles.

Making a rectangle from three triangles.

Joining diamonds.

wrong side

right side

Matching points on seams exactly.

LEFT The Carolina Lily Block is a combination of piecing and appliqué.

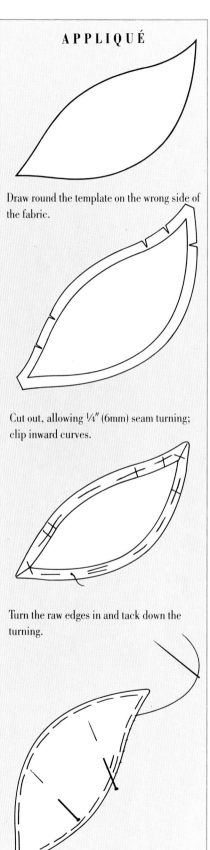

APPLIQUÉ

Draw round the template on the wrong side of the fabric.

Cut out, allowing ¼″ (6mm) seam turning; clip inward curves.

Turn the raw edges in and tack down the turning.

Pin and tack, then stitch down.

signs. Sometimes one large image was made, a tree of life for example, sometimes a series of similar repeated blocks, as in the Baltimore brides' quilts.

The technique lends itself more to pictorial designs and curved shapes than to pieced patchwork which is characterized by geometric designs and straight seams. The two techniques of appliqué and piecing were often used together in quilt designs such as the Flower Basket and the Carolina Lily.

Appliqué templates are the actual size of the piece to be applied and the seam allowance, or turning, must be added as the fabric is cut. The templates can be drawn freehand, traced from patterns or made from cut and folded paper. Place the template face down on the back of the fabric, draw round it with a fabric marker and cut out adding ¼ in (6 mm) to turn under. The raw edges of the piece must be turned under before it is pinned and stitched to the background. Clip any inward curves to facilitate turning under the edge, up to but not beyond the marked

line, turn the edge under and press. Now position the piece on the background, pin and tack (baste) if necessary, then hem down with neat stitches using a thread that matches the piece. Where several pieces are used, in a picture for example, the edge of one piece may be overlapped by the edge of another. In this case it is not necessary to turn under the raw edges of the piece to be overlapped. When the pieces have been stitched down to the background, to reduce its thickness and make quilting easier cut away the background fabric behind the piece ¼ in (6 mm) from the sewing line with a pair of sharp scissors.

Borders

If your quilt design includes a border, this must be added as part of the quilt top. Plain borders can provide an area for an elaborate quilting design or they can balance and contain the patchwork. A pieced border should complement the patchwork blocks. Try to use multiples of the measurement units that are in the quilt.

BORDERS

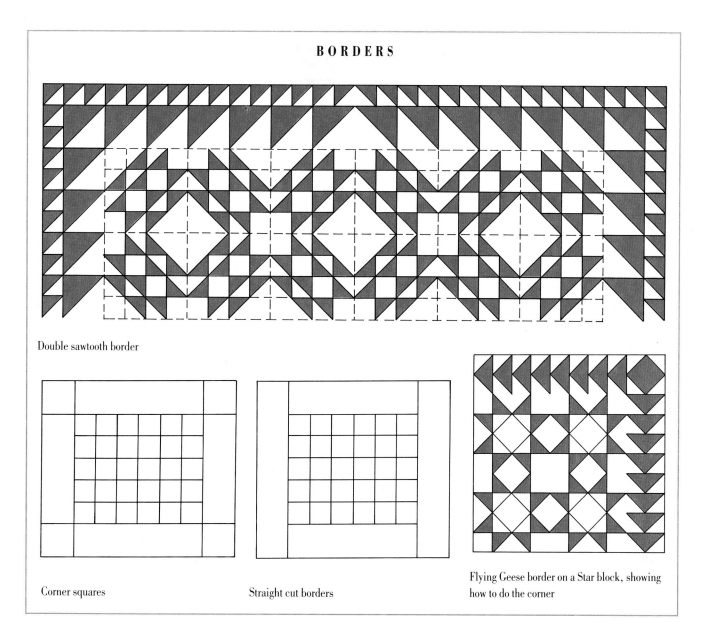

Double sawtooth border

Corner squares

Straight cut borders

Flying Geese border on a Star block, showing how to do the corner

Search the block pattern for border elements. A border, if included, should be an integral part of the quilt design, and not just added to make up the size.

STRAIGHT CUT BORDERS

Cut two strips to the length of the patchwork and the desired width, plus seam allowance, and stitch these to the sides. Now cut two more to match the width of the patchwork plus the added width of the long strips and join these to the top and the bottom.

CORNER SQUARES

This is a simple but effective border. Cut two strips to match the long sides of the patchwork and two strips to match the short sides, to the desired width plus seam allowance, and cut four squares the sides of which match the width of the border. Join two strips to the sides of the patchwork. Now add the corner squares to each end of the remaining strips and stitch these along the top and bottom, ensuring that the joins match.

MITRED CORNERS

For a border with mitred corners proceed as follows: cut the border strips to the desired width. The length of each strip should equal the length of the side of the patchwork, plus a generous allowance for the width of the border, which will allow for the mitres. Join the borders to the patchwork right sides together, and stop the stitching at the seam allowance at each corner. Place the quilt top right side down on a flat surface and fold one border over another and draw a straight line from the inner corner at an angle of 45° to the border. Reverse the positions of the borders and repeat. With the right sides of the borders together line up the marked seam lines and stitch from the inner to the outer corner. Before trimming away excess fabric, open the corner seam and press it to ensure it lies flat.

MITRED CORNERS

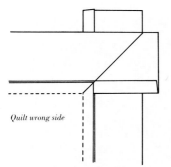

Quilt wrong side

Draw a straight line from the inner corner at a 45° angle.

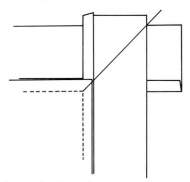

Reverse borders and repeat.

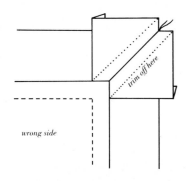

trim off here

wrong side

Stitch the borders together along the marked lines and press open. Trim away excess fabric.

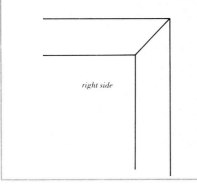

right side

LEFT & BELOW Quilting *by hand with a hoop*

~

OPPOSITE Part of a *Dresden Plate Block showing contour quilting.*

~

Assembling the Quilt

When piecing is complete, press the quilt top well; once the wadding (batting) and backing are attached ironing is not recommended as it will flatten the filler. If the top is bigger than the widest fabric available you will have to piece the backing and wadding, both of which should be 4 in (10 cm) bigger all round than the top. To join wadding butt the edges against each other and join with herringbone stitch edge to edge to avoid a ridge. Remove any selvedges from the backing before joining to make the size you need. Lay the backing wrong side up on a flat surface (on the floor if the quilt is large) and if possible tape it down. Smooth the wadding down gently on top, then the quilt top, being careful not to pull or stretch either as this may distort the quilt. Pin all three layers together, smoothing out wrinkles from the top and bottom. Starting from the centre, tack the three layers together easing excess fabric towards the edge. Cover the quilt with a grid of stitches 4–6 in (10–15 cm) apart.

Quilting

There are various ways of securing the three layers of the quilt together.

TIE QUILTING

For a quilt with a bulky filler such as 4-oz or 6-oz wadding (batting), or as a quick way to complete your quilt, tie quilting is ideal. Using thread in a strong natural fibre such as embroidery or crochet cotton, pull it through all three layers leaving an end long enough to tie (5 in/13 cm). Stitch again over the first stitch bringing the needle up near the loose end. Tie in a reef knot not too tightly as this might cause the fabric to tear. Trim the ends, or thread them into the quilt. Tie at regular intervals over the quilt surface, about 4–6 in (10–15 cm) apart. The knots can be used as decorative features either by themselves or in conjunction with buttons, beads or French knots.

HAND-QUILTING

Hand-quilting is done with small, even running stitches through the three layers of the quilt. A close web of quilting was necessary on old quilts to prevent the raw wool or cotton filler from bunching together at one end of the quilt, but with the bonded quilt wadding available today you can do as much or as little quilting as you like. Close quilting is still admired for the added texture it gives.

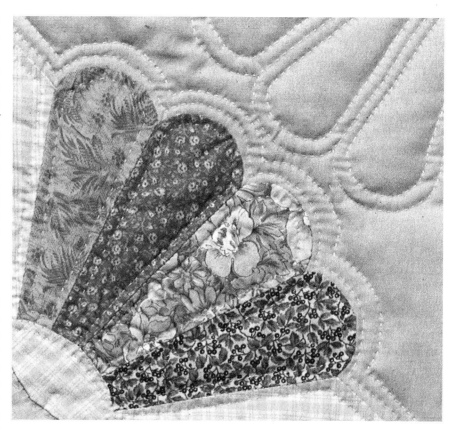

To hand quilt, take a length (about 16 in/40 cm) of single quilting thread and run it through bees wax, to strengthen the thread and help to prevent it knotting. Start with a knot and come up from the back of the quilt, tug the thread until the knot pops through the back. Try to keep stitches as even as possible; this is more important than their size. Quilting can be done on your lap, or you may prefer to use a hoop or frame. A quilting frame is a large and expensive item and if you have one you are probably already an experienced quilter. More accessible to the beginner is a hoop rather like an embroidery ring only larger – about 23 in (57 cm) in diameter. This may be on a stand, or can be rested against a table leaving both hands free. Keep the quilt fairly slack in the hoop and push the needle through from the top with a thimble worn on the middle finger of the sewing hand. Keep the other hand beneath the work to guide the needle back up. Expert quilters use a flat topped thimble on the lower hand, grazing the needle on the top

angle as they stitch, which ensures that each stitch has gone through all three layers. Take three to four running stitches with a rocking movement, keeping the thumb pressed down on the fabric just ahead of the stitching. To finish, tie a knot close to the last stitch and pull this through between the layers, bring the needle out at the front and cut the thread off.

Many quilt shows have demonstrations of quilting which are worth seeking out; an effective way of acquiring this skill.

QUILTING PATTERNS

Contour quilting A straightforward and traditional style of quilting, this echoes the shapes of the patches, which are outlined with a row of stitching ⅜ in (1 cm) from the seams. You can mark an even line with narrow masking tape or a fabric marker. Check on a scrap of fabric that any marks will come off.

Stencils Quilting designs form another study in themselves. Antique quilts have elaborate motifs which were marked on to the quilt top with stencils or drawn freehand by expert quilt-markers. Cables,

feathers and tulips were popular and together with geometric 'filler' patterns form highly decorative bas-relief surfaces on the quilt. Stencils are available in patchwork supply shops and can be used to mark out a quilting design. The quilt top should be marked before the three layers are assembled.

QUILTING BY MACHINE

If you plan to quilt by machine there are several points to consider. Tacking must be as thorough as for hand-quilting. Try to work out a quilting design which as far as possible runs in straight lines that do not cross. Turning a large quilt in the sewing machine is difficult; consider quilting larger items in two pieces and joining after quilting. To do this, when quilting is finished place the two halves right sides together and join through all thicknesses matching points where necessary. Trim away as much of the wadding as possible to reduce bulk, then pin a narrow strip of bias binding, matched to the backing, over the join and hem it to either side of the seam.

It is possible to buy a walking foot for some models of sewing-machine, and this attachment makes machine-quilting much easier. This is because it feeds the three layers of fabric through evenly rather than running the top layer forward, as does the standard foot, which may create small tucks. Keep the bulk of the quilt rolled up when you are not working on it and support it on the sewing-table. Mark quilting lines on the surface with a marker and try to match threads with the colour of the top where possible. Machine-quilting can be hidden in the seam. To do this press the fabric down as you work and open the seam to allow the needle to hit the centre or 'ditch' of the seam.

You can either start or finish with back stitches and clip off the threads, or pull all the threads through to the back and darn them into the quilt.

THREAD FOR MACHINE QUILTING
Use the type of thread you would normally use in your machine and match it to the quilt top where possible. Alternatively use invisible thread on top with thread to match the backing in the bobbin. The stitch length should be slightly longer (about 10–11 stitches per inch/25 mm) than for a seam.

If you have a machine that does decorative stitching, experiment with this to accent your machine quilting. A narrow

STRAIGHT BINDING

Cut the binding 2½″ (6cm) wide, and the length of the quilt edge.

Fold in half along the length and press.

Quilt right side

Pin and stitch the raw edges to the quilt on the right side. Stitch ¼″ (6mm) from edge.

Turn the folded edge of binding over to the wrong side of the quilt and hem it down.

ABOVE *Threads for*
machine quilting.
~

satin stitch with a multi-coloured thread forms the decorative focus on the block centres in 'log cabin windows', for example.

Final Finishing

When quilting is complete the edges must be neatened either by turning the raw edges of the quilt top and tacking to the inside and stitching together or putting a binding around the quilt to enclose the wadding (batting) and raw edges.

STRAIGHT BINDING
If a narrow binding is folded along its length before being stitched to the edges of the quilt, this makes a folded edge to turn over and enclose the raw edges and

wadding (batting) which is easily hemmed in place. This method makes it easier to get an even width of binding, giving the quilt a more professional finish. For the sides of the quilt cut two pieces of fabric on the straight grain to the desired length by 2½ in (6 cm) wide. Fold these strips in half along their length and press. There is now one side with two raw edges and one side with a fold. Place the side with raw edges along the top side of the quilt. Pin, tack (baste) and stitch through both layers of the binding and all layers of the quilt, taking in a ¼ in (6 mm) seam allowance. Turn the folded edge of the binding over the raw edges and hem down on the back of the quilt enclosing the wadding (batting). Repeat on the opposite side. For the

CORNERS

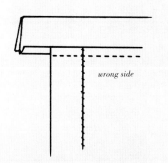

Leave ½″ (1.5cm) of binding beyond the edge.

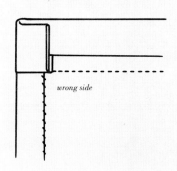

Turn up and press.

Turn the end in and press.

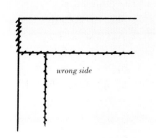

Turn the binding down over the wrong side of the quilt and hem down.

BIAS BINDING

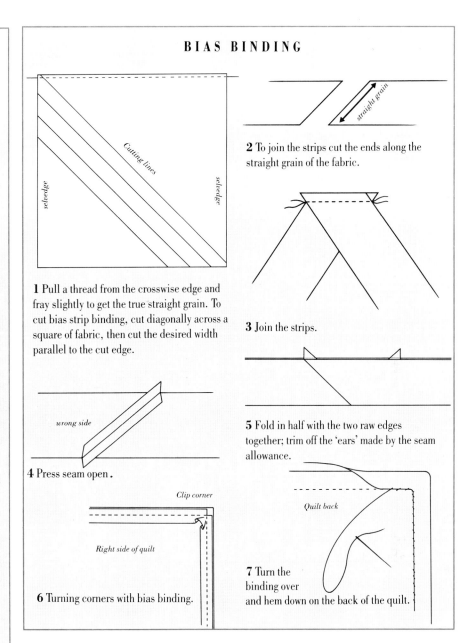

1 Pull a thread from the crosswise edge and fray slightly to get the true straight grain. To cut bias strip binding, cut diagonally across a square of fabric, then cut the desired width parallel to the cut edge.

4 Press seam open.

6 Turning corners with bias binding.

2 To join the strips cut the ends along the straight grain of the fabric.

3 Join the strips.

5 Fold in half with the two raw edges together; trim off the 'ears' made by the seam allowance.

7 Turn the binding over and hem down on the back of the quilt.

top and bottom leave ½ in (1.5 cm) of binding extending beyond the corners and neaten by turning in or mitring before final hemming.

BIAS BINDING

If a bias strip binding is used, it can be stitched all round the edges of the quilt continuously as the stretch in the bias cut of the material will ease round the corners. Measure the perimeter of your quilt and cut across the diagonal of the binding fabric in 2½ in (6.5 cm) wide strips. Join together enough pieces to accommodate the desired length using diagonal seams.

The bias strip is fairly stretchy so allow for this when estimating the length you need. Seam the ends of the binding pieces together to make a continuous ring. Press seams open then fold the binding in half with the wrong sides innermost. At this point you may trim off the 'ears' created by the seams. Pin the raw edges of the binding to the edge of the quilt on the top side. Tack and stitch with a ¼ in (6 mm) seam allowance. At the corners clip into the binding, but not past the seam allowance, to turn the corner more easily. Continue stitching around the corner. Turn the binding over the raw edge and hem.

Although it is more time-consuming than other methods, English patchwork does have certain advantages. It is possible to fit interlocking shapes together accurately, and if they are firmly stitched together, the result is a strong fabric. Curved pieces can be made, as in the Dresden Plate quilt, and then appliquéd on to a background. Of course, unless they are going to be combined with other shapes, it is a waste of time to stitch squares or rectangles together using this method. The American technique would be more suitable, and much less time-consuming.

Design

Try out different design layouts for hexagons, stars, diamonds and triangles on isometric graph paper. These shapes can be used singly or in combination. Isometric paper is marked out in a grid of triangles, and can also be used for making the papers which are tacked (basted) into the fabric patches, and for tracing accurate templates. Sort scrap fabrics into colour groups or tone values so that you can impose some order on your designs, or use a common fabric as a background or border. Although many English quilts are one-patch designs, that is, one shape is repeated, you can still work on the quilt in units rather than allowing it to grow so big as to be unwieldy.

DESIGNS ON ISOMETRIC GRAPH PAPER

Combining shapes over an isometric grid.

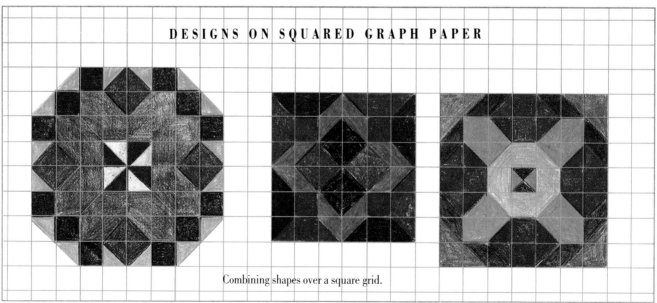

DESIGNS ON SQUARED GRAPH PAPER

Combining shapes over a square grid.

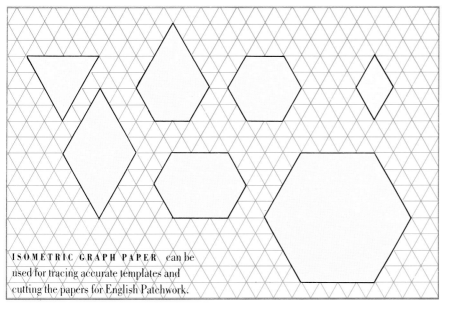

ISOMETRIC GRAPH PAPER can be used for tracing accurate templates and cutting the papers for English Patchwork.

SKETCH PLAN OF QUILT
on isometric graph paper

A sketch plan of the whole quilt can be made on isometric graph paper to provide a key to the layout and positioning of colour groups, dark and light areas and borders.

Grandmother's Flower Garden

Made of 19th-century dress cottons, this quilt is a straightforward interpretation of the flower garden design. Simple rosettes made of seven hexagons float in a field of acid green sprigged cotton which is also used for the border and backing. The restricted colour scheme of reddish browns and blue printed cotton give the quilt a calm and restful appeal. Striped and checked fabrics have been used in some of the rosettes and these form interesting focal points in the otherwise even texture of the surface. The quilting outlines the hexagons. Quilts with an 'antique' look are enjoying popularity at the moment; one American fabric manufacturer has revived some of the old dress prints from this era, and it is possible to buy preparations to artificially fade new quilts. Certainly, to attempt to reproduce a quilt like this would require careful selection of fabrics in a muted colour range, but the hexagonal shape is the least demanding in terms of sewing technique, so perseverance would be more important than skill in the production of such a quilt.

MATERIALS REQUIRED
Each rosette takes one piece of fabric 12 in × 8 in (30 cm × 20 cm) and a piece for the centre 4 in × 4 in (10 cm × 10 cm). There are 115 rosettes in the quilt top and 34 half rosettes around the edges.
▌For the background hexagons: 4½ yd (metres) of 45 in (115 cm) fabric.
▌Border and backing: 7 yd (metres).
▌Wadding (batting): the finished size of the quilt top, plus 4 in (10 cm) all round.
▌A hexagon template with 1–1½ in (3–4 cm) sides.
▌Paper for the backing papers.
Using the template, cut the papers and cover them with fabric, then make up the rosettes. If you make up all the rosettes first, then join them to the background fabric hexagons, you will

Granny's Garden

This quilt, made with hexagons using the English method of piecing, successfully bridges the gap separating contemporary quilt-making and the traditional Victorian mosaic quilts. It is composed of double rosettes of hexagons in mainly orange and earth tones, each with a yellow centre. These rosettes make creative use of the fabric prints, giving the quilt the same feel as an exquisite antique glass paperweight. Stripes radiate from and circle round the rosette centres. Printed squares set at random angles within some of the hexagons give the quilt a sense of movement, and the framing and placing of flower and paisley motifs demonstrate the skilled use of window templates. There is enough deliberate manipulation of tonal values in the centrally placed circle of lighter rosettes to give the design order, but the variety of fabrics used keeps the eye moving around the surface of the quilt

ABOVE: Back view of Grandmother's Flower Garden quilt using contemporary fabrics.
~

have more control over the placement of colours. Alternatively, if you begin connecting the rosettes when you have completed several, a more random arrangement can develop. Once a hexagon is surrounded completely, the paper can be removed and re-used several times. It appears that the edges of this quilt have been cut through the patchwork. in order to straighten them and attach the border, but other possibilities are suggested in chapter one. When the patchwork top and border is complete, assemble with the backing and wadding (batting) and quilt by outlining the hexagons. Finish with a narrow binding made from the border fabric, or turn the edges of the backing and border together and slip hem.

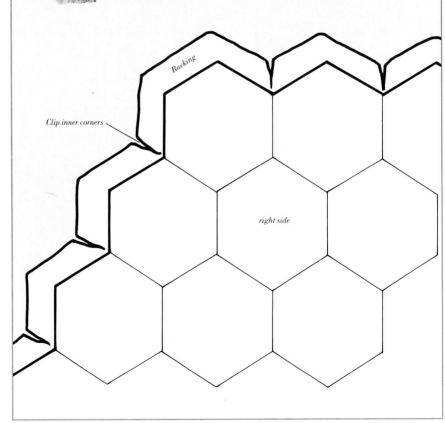

MAKING A SHAPED BACKING

Backing

Clip inner corners

right side

to investigate detail within that order. The final touch is in the border: by allowing the hexagons themselves to frame the quilt, the maker has not only dispensed with the problems of straightening the edge, but has projected her interpretation of the hexagon into contemporary focus. The quilting is done in bold, even stitches in hand-embroidery cotton. There is no wadding (batting) in the quilt.

MAKING A SHAPED BACKING

To shape the backing to the outer hexagons press the outer edges of the patchwork and carefully remove the papers. Cut the backing fabric, 1½ in (3.5 cm) larger than the quilt top all round, and tack (baste) the top and backing together with wrong sides facing. Trim the backing fabric round the shaped edge ⅜ in (9 mm) larger all round. Clip the inner corners on

ABOVE Granny's
Garden Quilt
~

the backing fabric so that when turned in it will lie flat against the back of the patchwork. Turn in the backing so that the folded edges of the patchwork and backing match up, pin, tack (baste) and slip hem the edges together. Quilt and remove tacking.

The first quilts made by the American pioneers were designed more for warmth than beauty. In the harsh winters every available resource had to be conserved and, where possible, re-cycled. Clothes and bedclothes were used and re-used, including being made into the first crazy quilts – a haphazard arrangement of fabric scraps stitched together and filled with anything, often more re-cycled fabrics such as blankets, that would insulate from the cold.

Despite the scarcity of fabrics it was not long before these early quilt-makers began to impose some order on the arrangement of colour and shapes. Simple one-patch designs such as Bricks or Hit and Miss were produced. These quilts could still make full use of available scraps but had an element of design.

The early settlers had limited living and working space, and they solved this problem by building their patchworks in units, or 'blocks'. Each block could be made individually and stacked away until there were enough to stitch together into a large sheet of patchwork to make up the quilt top. When 20 or 30 blocks were complete, the top was often quickly assembled and quilted as a cooperative effort at the 'quilting bee'.

Simple repeated designs were developed by folding squares of paper into first four, then nine equal parts, which were then sub-divided into geometric shapes. These were the beginnings of the block design, the unit on which American pieced patchwork is based. Made up in fabric, blocks can be used in a variety of different ways.

When blocks are placed edge to edge, secondary designs appear adding complexity to apparently simple block designs.

The blocks can be separated by strips of fabric, forming a lattice effect (sashing) over the quilt. This was often used on album quilts where each block is different and putting them edge to edge would result in a confusion of different shapes.

Set 'on point', the square blocks appear as diamonds. The edges of the quilt are filled with triangles to make up the square or rectangular shape.

Two or more block designs can be used together, which can create some intriguing

ABOVE & RIGHT Early American patchwork patterns like Bricks and Hit and Miss made full use of all available scraps of fabric.
~

secondary patterns; and a plain block used in conjunction with a patchwork block will provide an appropriate surface for elaborate quilting. Blocks are categorized by the number of equal parts into which they are divided. Four-patch and nine-patch are the most common, but there are numerous five- and seven-patch blocks. To determine which category a block falls into, impose a grid over the design. This will also help when deciding on the order of piecing; the rule is to start with the smallest pieces and work in straight lines where possible.

The colour and tonal values used in the block can radically affect its appearance. Decide which part of the block is to be

THE VERSATILITY OF
THE AMERICAN BLOCK

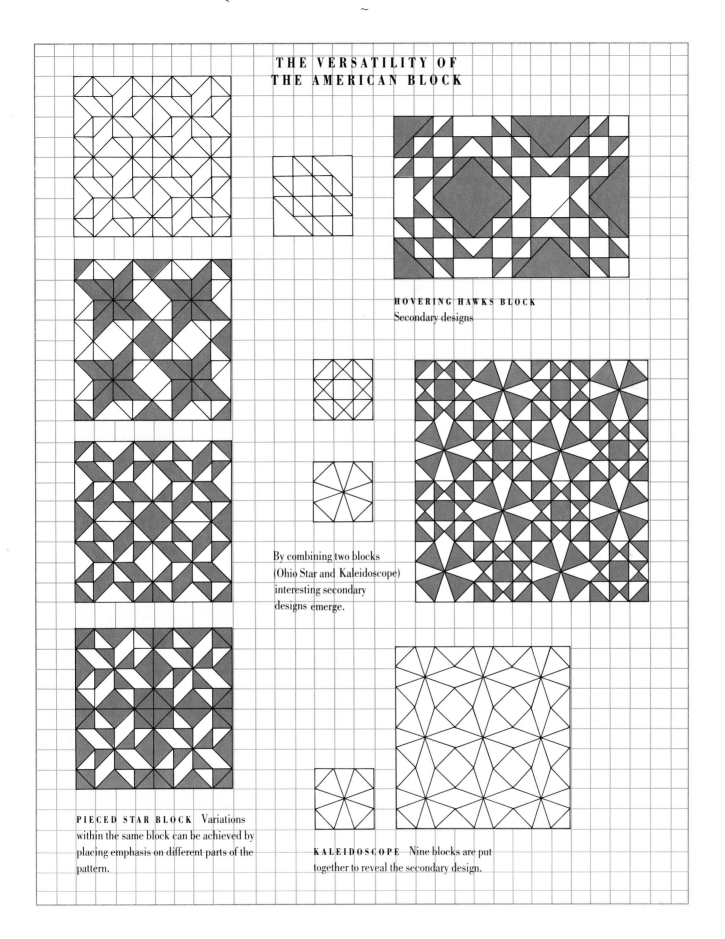

HOVERING HAWKS BLOCK
Secondary designs

By combining two blocks
(Ohio Star and Kaleidoscope)
interesting secondary
designs emerge.

PIECED STAR BLOCK Variations
within the same block can be achieved by
placing emphasis on different parts of the
pattern.

KALEIDOSCOPE Nine blocks are put
together to reveal the secondary design.

emphasized and use the strongest coloured fabrics on those shapes. Try shading in several versions of the same block in light, medium and dark before deciding on the position of the fabrics. Always put at least four blocks together in these drawings to reveal the secondary patterns. Some secondary patterns, eg the kaleidoscope, need at least six blocks together to show the full effect.

The basic principles of the repeat block provide a versatile way to approach quilt design. Even when simply reproducing a traditional pattern, variation and individuality can be achieved by your choice of fabrics, use of borders, and way of setting the blocks. Traditional blocks can be developed, or new ones invented within a basic grid. In the examples of block designs illustrated in this chapter, different approaches to design using the repeat block are explored.

ABOVE Castle Walls Quilt. Although each block in this quilt is the same pattern they look very different when emphasis is placed on different shapes in the block.
~
TOP LEFT Jack in the Box.
~
ABOVE LEFT Bear's Paw.
~

ALBUM QUILT WITH LATTICE STRIPS

*ABOVE Amish Churn
Dash quilt, detail.*

~

Amish Quilts

The Amish quilt-makers are notable for the graphic simplicity of their quilt designs. Working within the confines of their religious beliefs, which prescribe conformity to the 'plain' life-style and exclude any form of over-decoration including a one-time ban on patterned fabrics, they have created a stunning quilt style, recongnizable by the juxtaposing of pure colours combined with sombre browns, blues and black. Claims have been made that the abstract geometry of Amish quilts has played a significant part in the development of contemporary fine art.

The quilts are also renowned for their fine quilting, often using elaborate motifs such as rose, tulip, feather and cable. Today, antique Amish quilts are highly prized by collectors.

The Amish quilt illustrated here combines two blocks set on point. The patchwork block, sometimes known as Churn Dash, is a straightforward nine-patch and alternates with plain, closely quilted squares and triangles. A black band encloses the blocks, and the quilt is edged by a broad border in the same fabric as the plain background squares. The quilt is made in cotton and dates from the late 19th century.

Amish Churn Dash Quilt

Size 80 in × 70 in (203 cm × 178 cm)

MATERIALS REQUIRED
Fabric quantities based on 45 in (115 cm) wide fabric –
■ For the border and plain blocks: 3½ yd (metres).
■ Backing fabric: 5 yd (metres).
■ Wadding (batting): the finished size of the quilt plus 4 in (10 cm) all round.
■ Blocks: use the templates you make to calculate fabric amounts.

MAKING THE QUILT TOP
Being a simple nine-patch, this block design is one of the easiest and quickest to construct. As the blocks alternate with plain squares, construction of the top will be speeded up.
You may like to substitute one of the other block designs from the collection illustrated. Draw up the block on graph paper to the correct size and make templates. At this stage you must decide whether you are sewing by hand or machine as this will affect the templates.

The only difficulty with using the blocks set on point is in deciding which way to place the grain of the fabric. Make the blocks up with the fabric grain parallel to the sides of each block, and cut the side and corner triangles to be consistent with the blocks. Borders cut on the bias would cause too many problems with stretching and fitting, so cut them straight. This will help to contain the centre patchwork section. It is better to be flexible over the way you cut the fabric than to cause yourself extra problems by sticking rigidly to the rules. When all the blocks are made refer to the illustration and stitch them together in rows with a triangle at each end and on the corners. Stitch the rows together, matching the points between blocks. Before stitching on the borders run a line of stay stitching, that is, a straight line of running stitch, all round the edge of the patchwork to prevent it

stretching. Do this within the seam allowance so it will not show when the borders are attached. When the top is complete, assemble with the wadding (batting) and backing, and quilt and finish in the usual way.

Pinwheel Cot Quilt

A popular way of planning a scrap quilt is to use a common background fabric. In this small quilt, a plain, lavender-coloured cotton provides a uniform background to a variety of different patterned fabrics. It also unifies the design. The design of the block is a variation of the traditional Clay's Choice. (The comparison is made visually in the diagram below.) The blocks are made in such a way that when they are set edge to edge, they provide a secondary pattern which then turns the pinwheel

PINWHEEL BLOCKS

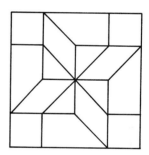

Clay's Choice – the traditional block.

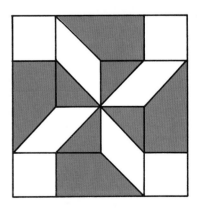

A variation used in pinwheel cot quilt. The width of the border strips is half that of each square in the block grid.

blades in opposite directions, giving the impression of spiralling movement. The plain shapes connecting the blocks are emphasized with machine quilting. The border of patterned strips is shaded through dark and light colours running gradually together. The edge of the quilt is finished with a patchwork bias binding. Quilting is done by machine using a narrow satin stitch in decorative embroidery thread, and the centre of each block is tied with a knot of hand-embroidery cotton.

The block size is 8 in (20 cm), and the border strips are 1 in × 3 in (2.5 cm × 8 cm). The overall size of the quilt is 30 in × 39 in (76 cm × 99 cm).

MATERIALS REQUIRED
Based on 45 in (115 cm) wide fabric –
- For the blocks: 24 pieces of patterned fabric each 9 in × 6 in (23cm × 15 cm).
- For the background: ¾ yd (metre) of plain fabric.
- Backing: 1½ yd (metre).
- 2 oz wadding (batting).
- Machine-embroidery thread. Madeira shaded, colour number 2103, one 500-metre reel was used on this quilt, though any other shaded or plain thread to your own taste can be used.
- For the border: small pieces of fabric from your scrap bag.
- Draw and make the templates for the blocks. Three shapes are required: a square, a triangle and a rhomboid.

CUTTING OUT
Each block requires two patterned fabrics and the plain background fabric.

From the first patterned fabric cut four rhomboids. When cutting out, note that the rhomboid shape is not symmetrical so the template must be placed face down on the wrong side of the fabric.

From the second patterned fabric cut four squares.

From the plain fabric cut four squares and eight triangles.

PIECING
Follow the order of piecing outlined above. Join the blocks together 3 across and 4 down.

ABOVE *Pinwheel cot quilt.*

~

THE BORDER
Each strip in the border is half as wide as one of the grid squares in the block, so eight strips fit along one side of the block.

Make a template the correct width for your block and the desired length. For the 8 in (20 cm) block, the strips are 1 in × 3 in (2.5 cm × 8 cm) finished size. The sides of the corner squares measure the same as the long sides of the border strips.

Piece the border strips: 24 strips for each of the shorter edges and 32 for each of the longer edges. Add the corner squares to each end of the shorter borders. Stitch the borders to the longer sides first, then to the shorter sides, taking care to match the points at the corners.

QUILTING
Mark the quilting lines in the plain areas between the blocks, ¾ in (2 cm) from the seams, with a fabric marker. Assemble the quilt top, wadding (batting) and backing and tack (baste) thoroughly. Stitch along the marked lines to quilt, first with straight stitch and then with a narrow satin stitch (about number 2 on the sewing

PIECING ORDER

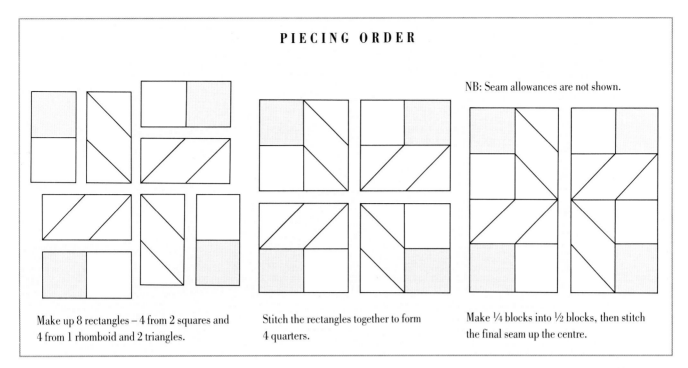

NB: Seam allowances are not shown.

Make up 8 rectangles – 4 from 2 squares and 4 from 1 rhomboid and 2 triangles.

Stitch the rectangles together to form 4 quarters.

Make ¼ blocks into ½ blocks, then stitch the final seam up the centre.

TEMPLATE FOR PATCHWORK BIAS BINDING

The seam allowance has been added to the template.

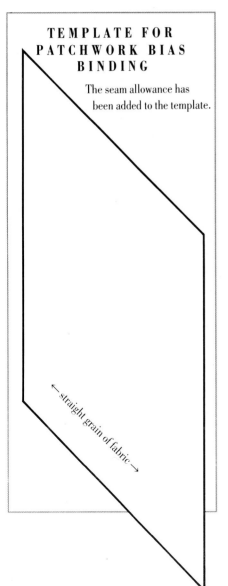

← straight grain of fabric →

machine) in decorative thread. Satin stitch over the join between the border and the blocks. Quilt round and between the patterned squares with a matching thread in the ditch of the seams. Tie a knot at the centre of each block with embroidery thread to match the patterned fabric.

PIECED BIAS BINDING

The bias binding is also patchwork, rather than a continuous length in one fabric. To make the patchwork bias binding, trace the template (the seam allowance has been added to the template so do not add it when cutting fabric). Now measure the perimeter of your quilt and cut enough pieces of different fabrics to give you this length. (Plan the fabrics and colours before you cut.) Remember that the bias binding is fairly stretchy, so allow for this. Seam the pieces together on the straight grain edges (ie, the short sides), taking ¼ in (6 mm) seam allowance, and join them into a continuous ring. Press all the seams open, then press the binding in half along its length with the wrong side innermost. It is now double, with two raw edges on one side and a fold on the other. Trim off the seam allowance ends that project beyond the raw edges. Now attach the binding to the quilt.

PATCHWORK BIAS BINDING

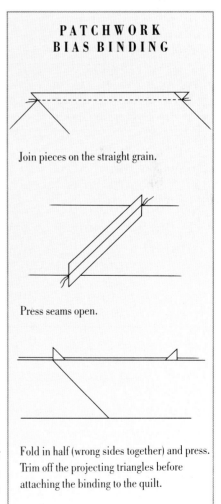

Join pieces on the straight grain.

Press seams open.

Fold in half (wrong sides together) and press. Trim off the projecting triangles before attaching the binding to the quilt.

Dictionary of Block Designs
The block designs are arranged in three sets of nine. The blocks in the first set are made only of squares and triangles and are easy to piece. The second set intro- duces another shape – the rhomboid – but with care should not present any problems. The third set of blocks is quite difficult and is recommended for the more experi- enced patchworker.

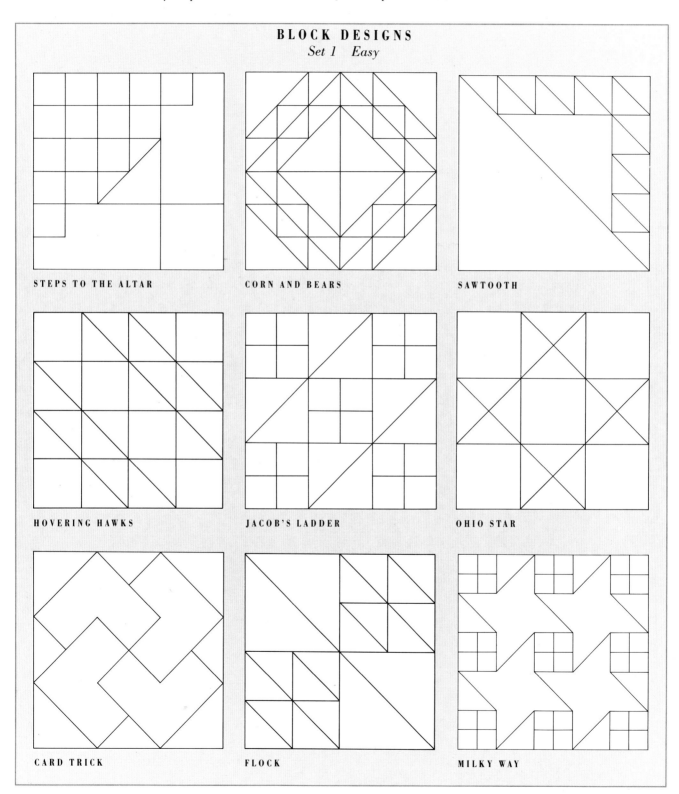

BLOCK DESIGNS
Set 1   Easy

STEPS TO THE ALTAR

CORN AND BEARS

SAWTOOTH

HOVERING HAWKS

JACOB'S LADDER

OHIO STAR

CARD TRICK

FLOCK

MILKY WAY

BLOCK DESIGNS
Set 2 Moderately easy

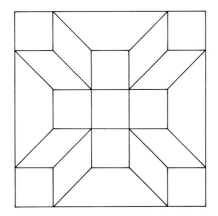

FARMER'S DAUGHTER

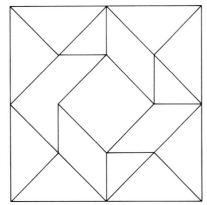

WINDBLOWN SQUARE

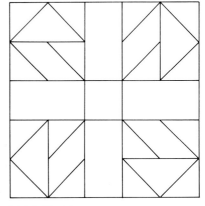

JACK IN THE BOX

ROLLING PINWHEEL

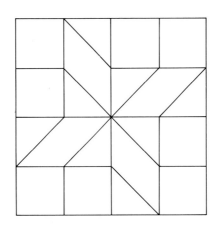

CLAY'S CHOICE

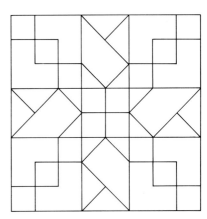

ARROWHEADS

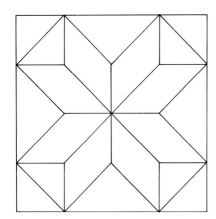

PIECED STAR

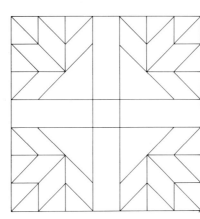

GOOSE TRACKS

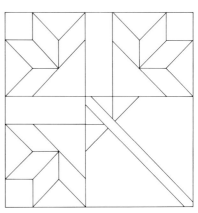

LILY

BLOCK DESIGNS
Set 3 Difficult

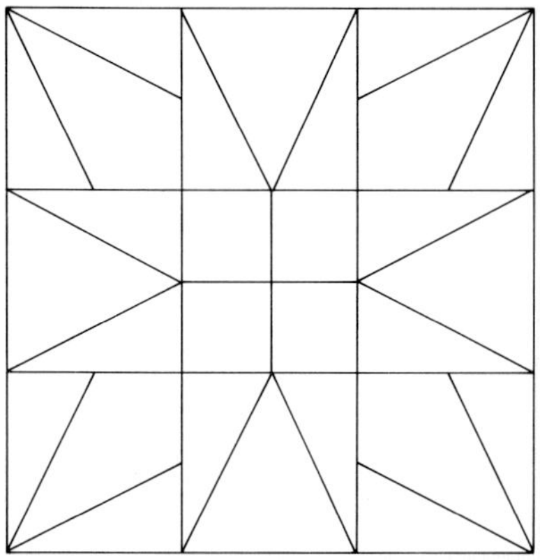

CLAWS

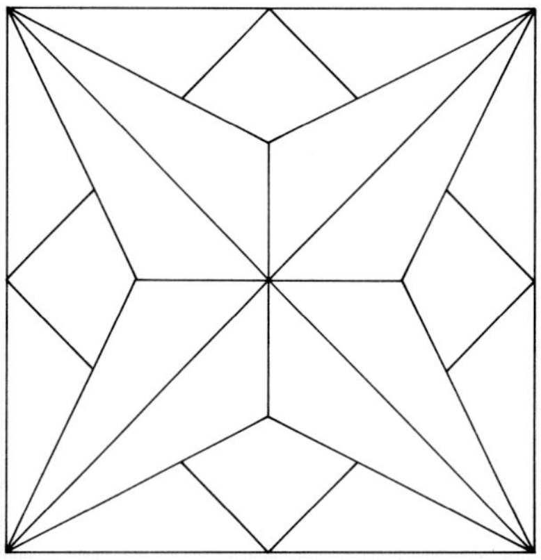

STAR

EASTERN STAR

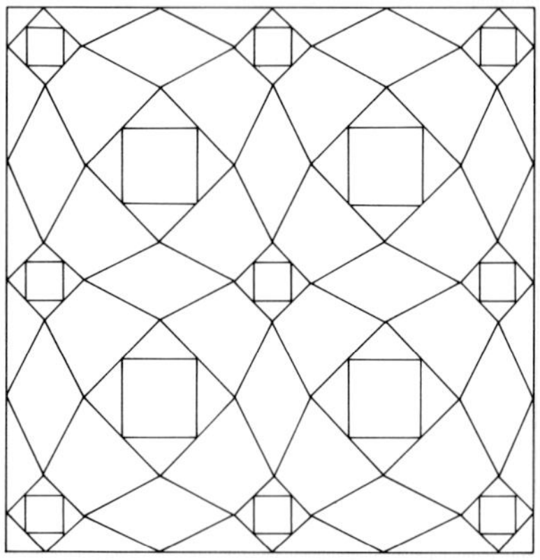

STORM AT SEA

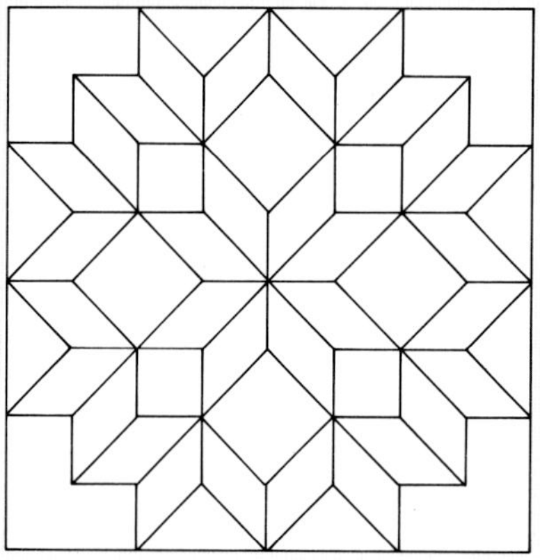

DUTCH ROSE

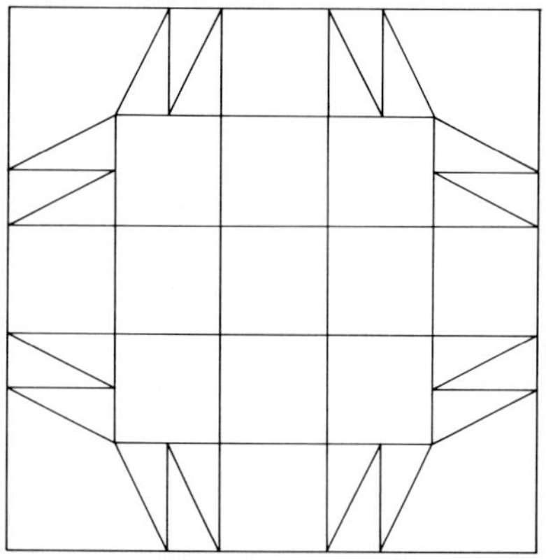

PIGEON TOES

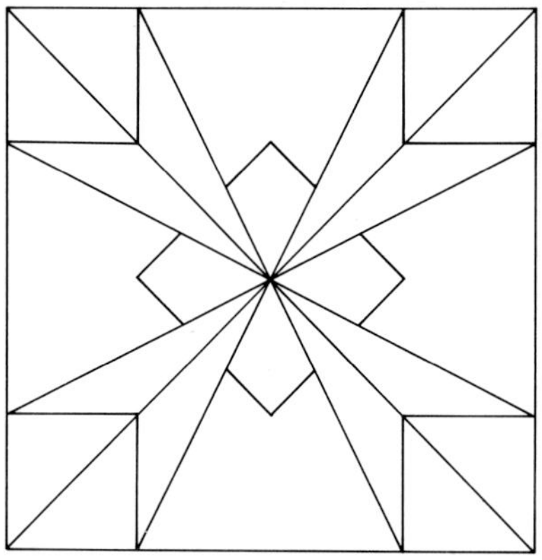

DOUBLE STAR

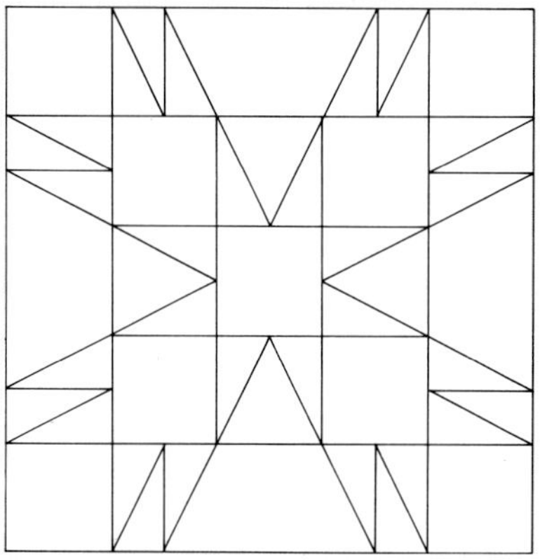

ST LOUIS STAR

DOVE IN THE WINDOW

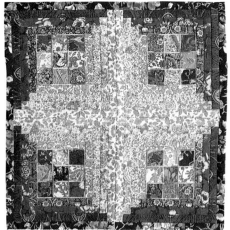

ABOVE, RIGHT & OPPOSITE
The Log Cabin block has the potential for a wide variety of designs: Barn Raising (this page)

~

Among the traditional quilt designs, log cabin ranks as one of the favourites. This may be due in large part to its familiarity: even people who have little knowledge of quilt designs seem to recognize a log cabin quilt. However, another underlying reason may be that it symbolizes the settlement of a continent, representing home in a hostile environment. Although log cabin quilts were made in Europe, the design is largely associated with the United States and the early settlers, and this enduring quilt pattern has maintained its popularity up until the present day.

Examine the construction of a single log cabin block and you will find it quite straightforward; strips of fabric rotate around a centre square which was traditionally red, to represent the fire or hearth. The block is split diagonally into light and dark fabrics to create the illusion of shadows and flickering firelight within the cabin.

There are many variations in the construction of the log cabin block, but they all rely on this visual play of light and dark tonal values. The blocks can be set together to produce an extraordinary variety of designs, three of the favourites being barn raising, straight furrow and courthouse steps. The size of the basic block can be changed by varying the width of the strips or the size of the centre square.

BASIC LOG CABIN BLOCK –
Shading and Numbered Sequence of Stitching

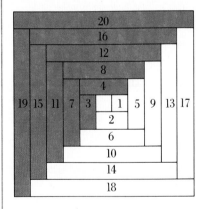

LOG CABIN BLOCK spiral arrangement of strips

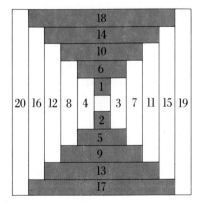

COURT HOUSE STEPS In this variation strips are sewn either side of the centre square

Traditional Log Cabin Quilt

This traditional log cabin quilt is made up of English printed dress cottons and dates from about 1860. The blocks are made in the spiral method, each one having five rounds of strips around the centre square. They are set together with the dark and light sides of each block set opposite each other, which creates strong diagonal lines moving across the quilt surface. The size of the quilt is approximately 80 in (200 cm) by 96 in (242 cm). Thirty 16 in (41 cm) blocks are needed for a quilt this size.

MATERIALS REQUIRED

The log cabin is an ideal design for a scrap quilt, so a good collection of fabrics in pure cotton or polycotton is necessary. If you are buying new fabrics, eleven different ones are needed for the quilt top; five in light and five in dark tones and one for the centre squares in the following amounts, calculated on 45 in (115 cm) wide fabric:

▪ For the centre square – ½ yd (metre)
Strips 1 & 2 – ½ yd (metre) light
Strips 3 & 4 – ½ yd (metre) dark
Strips 5 & 6 – ¾ yd (metre) light
Strips 7 & 8 – ¾ yd (metre) dark
Strips 9 & 10 – 1 yd (metre) light
Strips 11 & 12 – 1 yd (metre) dark
Strips 13 & 14 – 1 yd (metre) light
Strips 15 & 16 – 1¼ yd (metre) dark
Strips 17 & 18 – 1¼ yd (metre) light
Strips 19 & 20 – 1½ yd (metre) dark

▪ The size of the completed quilt top is 96 in × 80 in (242 cm × 200 cm), so a piece of cotton backing 100 in × 84 in (2.60 m × 2.10 m) and a piece of wadding (batting) the same size are required.

METHOD OF CONSTRUCTION

For a 16 in (41 cm) block made up of five rounds of strips, the finished size of the centre square needs to be 3½ in (9 cm) across, and the strips need to be 1¼ in (32 mm) wide, so add ¼ in (6 mm) seam allowance all round when cutting out. Cut fabric for the centre square 4 in × 4 in (10 cm × 10 cm) and the strips 1¾ in (4.5 cm) wide. This block can be made by hand or machine; a running stitch ¼ in (6 mm) from the cut edge is used to stitch fabrics together.

PREPARATION

Sort fabrics into light and dark values; plain or patterned fabrics can be used, or a combination of the two. The important point is to have two contrasting groups of fabrics.

Cut the strips on the straight grain of the fabric either lengthwise or crosswise. Mark the strips by drawing directly onto the fabric with a fabric marker. If you are using new fabric a rotary cutter and board will speed up cutting. Cut

LOG CABIN BLOCK CONSTRUCTION SEQUENCE

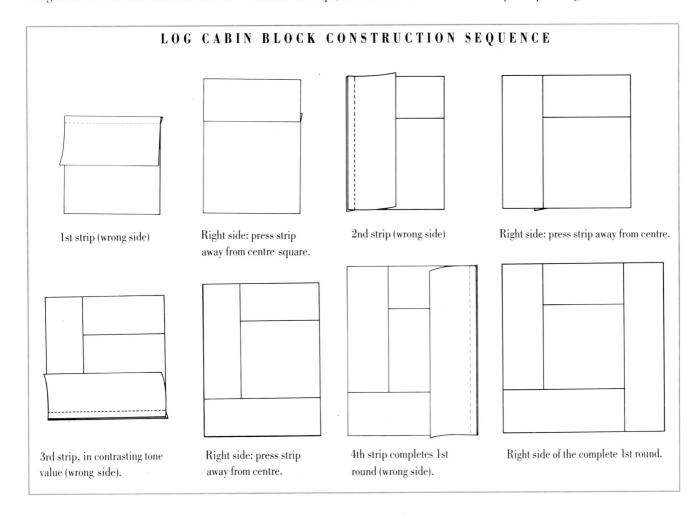

1st strip (wrong side)

Right side: press strip away from centre square.

2nd strip (wrong side)

Right side: press strip away from centre.

3rd strip, in contrasting tone value (wrong side).

Right side: press strip away from centre.

4th strip completes 1st round (wrong side).

Right side of the complete 1st round.

the strips accurately, as any inaccuracy in cutting out will transfer itself to the stitching, and then to the finished blocks, it will create blocks of unequal sizes, and cause difficulty in fitting them together, resulting ultimately in unevenness in the appearance of the overall quilt design.

There are no points to match in the log cabin block, and if accuracy is carefully maintained in the cutting and stitching this is an easy one to construct.

MAKING UP THE BLOCKS

Cut the centre squares; they should measure 4 in by 4 in (10 cm by 10 cm). Then select the fabric to be used for the first strip. Cut a length to fit the side of the square and pin right sides together. Stitch ¼ in (6 mm) from the edge. On the wrong side press the seam towards the strip. Using the same fabric for strip 2,

cut another length to fit the edge of the square plus the added width of strip 1. Pin, stitch and press as before.

The third and fourth strips are cut from the contrasting tone-value group. Cut strip 3 the length of the square plus the edge of strip 2; pin, stitch and press. The fourth strip completes the first round.

Continue adding strips, increasing the length of each to accommodate the width of the previous strip, and placing light and dark fabrics in the correct sequence. The strips can rotate in a clockwise or anti-clockwise direction, but must be consistent in all blocks and not change direction.

When you have made 30 blocks lay them together using the picture as a guide and stitch, taking in ¼ in (6 mm) seam allowance. Stitch the blocks together in groups of four or six first, rather than in long

lines. If they are slightly different sizes, the longer the seams the more difficult it becomes to match points between the blocks. By stitching together in groups of four or six, any slight inaccuracies in size can be eased to fit. Press open the seams between the blocks as matching points is easier with open seams.

The patchwork top is now complete. In the antique quilt illustrated there is no border; the block setting extends to the edge of the quilt. Alternatively, a narrow binding would be an appropriate way to finish this quilt.

Assemble the quilt top, wadding (batting) and backing as described in the section on basic methods and quilt by hand or machine.

*LEFT Diamond Log
Cabin quilt.*
~

The Diamond Log
Cabin Quilt

The Blazing Star design was one favoured by the expert needlewoman to show off her skills in a masterpiece quilt, and the graphic qualities of this design are added to those of the Log Cabin by altering the shape of the block centres in this quilt. The blocks are constructed in the same way as the square log cabin, with strips rotating around a central piece, but the central piece is a diamond rather than a square. The same principles of light and shade manipulation are used to dynamic effect. When the blocks are set together in a large six-pointed star, with the dark sides of the block innermost, a pattern of radiating hexagons emerges. The red diamond centres of each of the fifty-four blocks pivot the eye around the star shape. The possible problem of fitting this shape into a final frame has been solved by making the quilt a large hexagon, filling the negative space with six plain diamonds which reflect each segment of the centre star. A striped border of darker fabrics edges the quilt. The centre-star shape is tied rather than quilted so there is no surface stitch-ing to detract from the central pattern, whilst the outer diamonds are closely quilted by machine. The size of the quilt is approximately 100 in (260 cm) wide.

MATERIALS REQUIRED
Based on 45 in (115 cm) wide fabric –
▌For the centre diamonds – ½ yd (metre)
  Strips 1 & 2 – ½ yd (metre) light
  Strips 3 & 4 – ½ yd (metre) dark
  Strips 5 & 6 – ½ yd (metre) light
  Strips 7 & 8 – ½ yd (metre) dark
  Strips 9 & 10 – ½ yd (metre) light
  Strips 11 & 12 – ½ yd (metre) dark

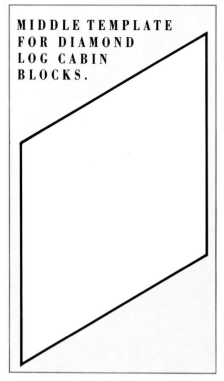

MIDDLE TEMPLATE FOR DIAMOND LOG CABIN BLOCKS.

Strips 13 & 14 – ½ yd (metre) light
Strips 15 & 16 – ½ yd (metre) dark
▌For the border – ¾ yd (metre) of each fabric to be used.
▌For the large plain diamonds – 2½ yd (metre) of 60 in (150 cm) wide fabric.
▌Wadding (batting) 100 in (2.60 m) square.

MAKING UP THE BLOCKS

Trace the centre template and cut out the diamond centres in your chosen fabric. The finished width of the strips is ½ in (13 mm) so cut them 1 in (25 mm) wide to allow a ¼ in (6 mm) seam allowance each side. The first two strips are light coloured. Lay a strip along one side of the diamond centre with the right sides together, leaving enough fabric each end to trim to the correct angle after stitching. Stitch, taking in a ¼ in (6 mm) seam allowance. On the wrong side press the seam towards the diamond centre and trim the ends of the strip in line with the sides of the diamond, maintaining the correct angle. Add strip 2 in the same light fabric, stitch, press and trim as before.

Strips 3 and 4 are dark coloured. Add the third strip stitching, pressing and trimming as before.

ABOVE A Blazing Star quilt, machine pieced and hand quilted, made of cotton and other fabrics.
~
BELOW Front and back views of a single Diamond Log Cabin block.
~

Strip 4 completes the first round of strips. Continue to add strips keeping the light and dark fabrics in sequence until four rounds have been completed. Fifty-four log cabin blocks are required for the six-pointed star.

JOINING THE BLOCKS

Begin by making the six sections of the star from nine blocks each. In order to join diamond shapes together, the seam allowance, rather than the cut edge, needs to be aligned, so that when the diamonds are opened out flat after stitching you have a straight edge.

Join rows of three blocks and press seams open at this stage. Then, matching seams, join the rows of three to produce a large diamond made up of nine blocks. Remember to keep the darker sides of the blocks all pointing one way.

Before joining the star points together, make a template from one of them for the plain diamonds. Join the sections in two sets of three, darker sides of the blocks innermost, then put the two halves together and stitch the final seam across the centre of the star. Leave a ¼ in (6 mm) unstitched at each inner angle of the star. Press these seams open.

Carefully position the six plain diamonds between the star points, then pin and stitch. At the inner angle of the points, turn the plain diamonds through the unstitched seam allowance. Press the plain diamond seam towards the star.

THE BORDER STRIPS

Using the darker fabrics cut a series of strips 1½ in (4 cm) wide and the length of each of the six sides. By having fewer or more strips, or altering the widths, the size of the quilt can be adjusted. Work around the edge of the quilt, trimming the ends of the strips to fit the angle of the hexagon. Save the final, outer strip as a binding to enclose wadding and backing. Make sure you cut the backing when the final strip is on, to achieve the right size for it. Assemble the quilt, tack (baste), tie the coloured part and quilt the outer, white parts by hand or machine.

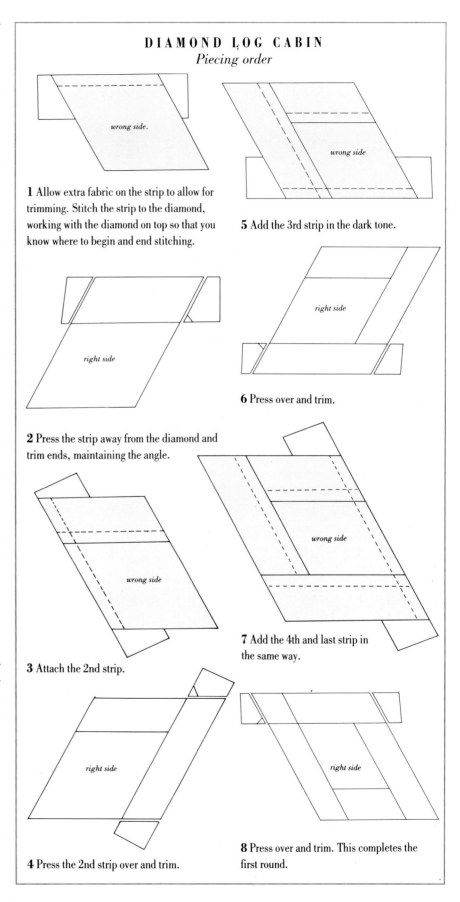

DIAMOND LOG CABIN
Piecing order

1 Allow extra fabric on the strip to allow for trimming. Stitch the strip to the diamond, working with the diamond on top so that you know where to begin and end stitching.

2 Press the strip away from the diamond and trim ends, maintaining the angle.

3 Attach the 2nd strip.

4 Press the 2nd strip over and trim.

5 Add the 3rd strip in the dark tone.

6 Press over and trim.

7 Add the 4th and last strip in the same way.

8 Press over and trim. This completes the first round.

JOINING THE DIAMOND BLOCKS TOGETHER

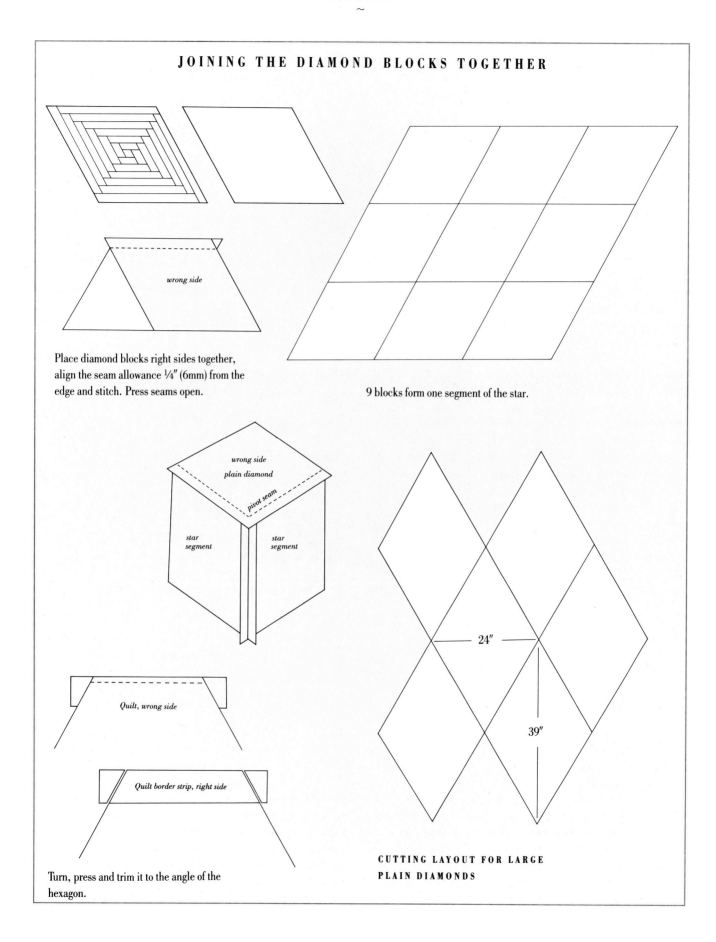

wrong side

Place diamond blocks right sides together, align the seam allowance ¼″ (6mm) from the edge and stitch. Press seams open.

9 blocks form one segment of the star.

wrong side
plain diamond
pivot seam
star segment
star segment

Quilt, wrong side

Quilt border strip, right side

Turn, press and trim it to the angle of the hexagon.

24″

39″

CUTTING LAYOUT FOR LARGE PLAIN DIAMONDS

Log Cabin Windows

This quilt is a contemporary interpretation of the traditional log cabin block, set in the 'light and dark' or 'sunshine and shadow' variation. Each set of four blocks has the lighter sides set together making strong, light diamonds. The red fabrics used on the dark sides of the centre blocks are carried half-way into the edging and corner blocks, giving a diffused appear-

ABOVE Log Cabin Windows.

~

ance to the centre of the quilt. The viewer has to look closely into the quilt's surface at first to identify the secondary, darker diamonds, but once established the dark and light diamonds seem to shift, increasing the impression of a garden glimpsed through tiny windows. This is created by

the block centres, which are not a plain square, but a tiny nine-patch of floral fabric embroidered with satin stitch in a multi-coloured thread.

The 'logs' or strips of each block are folded and applied to a base fabric giving the quilt added surface texture. This is a development of the technique used in some old log cabin quilts where the pieced fabric was stitched onto squares of backing, thereby dispensing with the need for a filler. Once the quilt top is completed all that is needed is a backing sheet to conceal the seams. This folding and stitching makes a rather heavy quilt which is therefore more suitable for a wall hanging or throw than for use as a bedspread.

MATERIALS REQUIRED

The same principles apply as for other log cabin quilts. This is a scrap quilt so a good selection of light and dark fabrics is needed, and because they are to be folded, cotton lawn is ideal; its light weight and close weave make it easy to handle and fine enough to take the folding without becoming too heavy.

■ You also need 2½ yd (metre) of bonda-web which is ½ yd (metre) wide. Bonda-web is a fabric glue bonded onto a paper backing. It is placed against the wrong side of the fabric with the glue side, which feels slightly rougher than the paper side, face down, and ironed on. The paper can then be peeled away leaving a patch of fabric glue to which other fabrics can be bonded with a medium iron.

■ For the base squares: 3¼ yd (metre) of white cotton sheeting 60 in (150 cm) wide.
■ Backing material: a piece of cotton 64 in (155 cm) square.
■ Machine embroidery thread: Madeira multi-coloured shade 2103, 500 metre reel was used on this quilt, although any other plain or shaded thread can be used.
■ Sewing-machine with a swing needle.

There are 64 blocks in the quilt made up in sets of four; ie, each set of blocks is made up in the same sequence of fabric for the strips, although the centres are different.

THE BLOCK CENTRES

Cut the sheeting into 10 in (26 cm) squares and find the centre point of each by ironing diagonal lines across. Draw a 5 in (13 cm) square in the centre. Cut a 5 in (13 cm) square of bondaweb and iron this onto the marked out square, then peel off the paper backing. Cut out the nine patches to the exact size of the templates given in the diagram. Lay the patches onto the 5 in (13 cm) square of bondaweb, overlapping

them very slightly (about 3 mm). This will prevent the raw edges lifting under the satin stitch. Now iron down the patches to stick them to the backing.

Satin stitch over the raw edges (you will find it easier to get a straight line if you do a row of straight stitching first) using the decorative thread. Now mark the 'frame' (see diagram) and stitch it in satin stitch also.

THE STRIPS

The strips are arranged in the spiral way. Although only ½ in (13 mm) of fabric is revealed on each strip, another ¾ in (19 mm) must lie under the next row of strips because the stitching is ½ in (13 mm) from the folded edges and must catch in the raw edges of the preceding row. The first two rounds of strips are therefore cut 2½ in (6.5 cm) wide, then folded in half lengthwise and pressed to give the correct final width of the strip.

FIRST ROUND

Remember that the blocks are worked four at a time. Select fabric for strips 1 and 2 from the light values. Strip 1 is 5 in (13 cm) long and strip 2 is 5½ in (14 cm) long, so for four blocks, cut a strip total-ling 42 in long by 2½ in wide (107 cm by 6.5 cm). Fold the fabric in half lengthwise and press, then mark the stitching line ½ in (13 mm) from the folded edge. Divide it into four lengths of 5 in (13 cm) for the first side, and four more 5½ in (14 cm) long for the second side. Take a 5 in

ABOVE Detail showing
folded strips.
~

(13 cm) strip and place the folded edge against the 'window-frame' on the block centre. Pin and stitch along the line marked ½ in (13 mm) from the folded edge. Use matching thread. Repeat on the other three blocks.

Now give the block a quarter turn and place a 5½ in (14 cm) strip against the frame stitching on the second side and across the end of the first strip. Stitch ½ in (13 mm) from the folded edge along the marked line. Repeat on the other three blocks.

Strips 3 and 4 are in dark values. Select the fabric and for four blocks cut a length of 46 in long by 2½ in wide (117 cm by 6.5 cm). Press in half as before, mark a stitching line ½ in (13 mm) from the folded edge and divide into four pieces 5½ in (14 cm) long, and four 6 in (15.5 cm) long. Place a 5½ in (14 cm) strip against the frame stitching on the third side of the window and stitch as before using match-ing thread. Position a 6 in (15.5 cm) strip on the fourth side and stitch along the marked line. Repeat on the other three blocks.

The first round is now complete. The corner and side patches of the central square will have been reduced to the same size as the centre patch, and the stitching will have caught the raw edges of the patches, leaving a ½ in (13 mm) fold free.

Templates and layout for miniature nine-patch block centres for 'LOG CABIN WINDOWS' quilt.

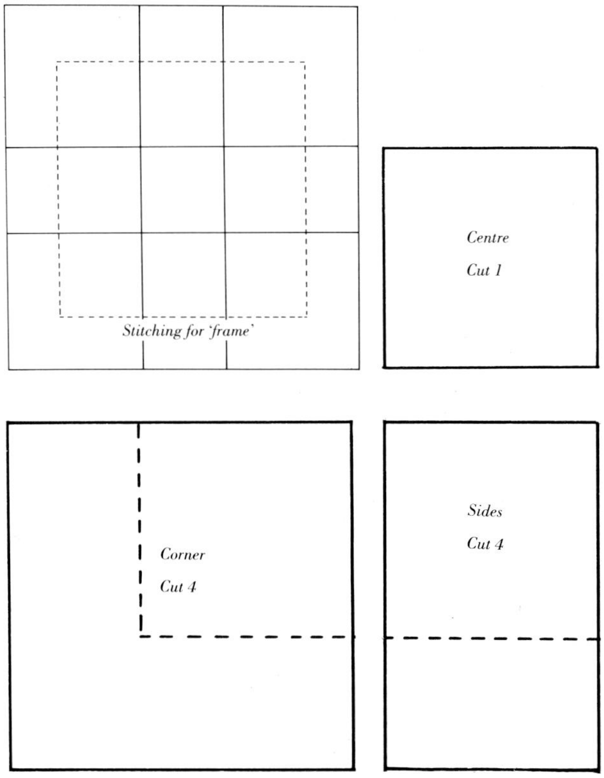

Stitching for 'frame'

Centre
Cut 1

Corner
Cut 4

Sides
Cut 4

ABOVE

Log Cabin Windows Block. Stage 1 showing the centre patches and decorative stitching.

~

SECOND ROUND

Prepare the fabric for the second round as for the first round. Strips 5 and 6 are in a light fabric and are 6 in (15.5 cm) and 6½ in (16.5 cm) long. Strips 7 and 8 are in a dark fabric and are 6½ in (16.5 cm) and 7 in (18 cm) long. Cut, fold and press them, and mark the stitching line. Position them against the stitching on the first round, and attach along the stitching line, rotating the block as before.

THIRD ROUND

We must now look ahead to the fourth round of strips. The fourth round lies flat against the backing, instead of being folded, in order to reduce bulk when joining the blocks together. This affects the third round of strips as the extra ¾ in (1.9 cm) beyond the stitching lines as on rounds 1 and 2 is not necessary, strip 4 requiring only ¼ in (6 mm) seam allowance.

The third round of strips should be cut 1½ in (4 cm) wide, which when folded in half will give ¾ in (19 mm) wide strips. All the strips in round three are 7¼ in (18.5 cm) long, so for the four blocks cut a length 58 in long by 1½ in wide (148 cm by 4 cm) from light fabric and 58 in long by 1½ in wide (148 cm by 4 cm) from dark fabric. Fold the strips in half, press and mark the stitching line ½ in (13 mm) from the fold and divide each length into

CHART OF MEASUREMENTS FOR FOLDED STRIPS						
	STRIP NO.	WIDTH		LENGTH		TONE VALUE
ROUND 1	1	2½in	6.5cm	5in	13cm	light
	2	2½in	6.5cm	5½in	14cm	light
	3	2½in	6.5cm	5½in	14cm	dark
	4	2½in	6.5cm	6in	15.5cm	dark
ROUND 2	5	2½in	6.5cm	6in	15.5cm	light
	6	2½in	6.5cm	6½in	16.5cm	light
	7	2½in	6.5cm	6½in	16.5cm	dark
	8	2½in	6.5cm	7in	18cm	dark
ROUND 3	9	1½in	4cm	7¼in	18.5cm	light
	10	1½in	4cm	7¼in	18.5cm	light
	11	1½in	4cm	7¼in	18.5cm	dark
	12	1½in	4cm	7¼in	18.5cm	dark
ROUND 4	13	1¼in	3.5cm	7½in	19cm	light
	14	1¼in	3.5cm	8in	20.5cm	light
	15	1¼in	3.5cm	8½in	21.5cm	dark
	16	1¼in	3.5cm	9in	23cm	dark

ABOVE RIGHT
Log Cabin Windows
Block. Stage 3, three
rounds of strips in
position.
~

RIGHT
Log Cabin Windows –
one completed block.
~

eight equal strips. Place the fold of each strip against the previous line of stitching on round 2 and stitch down strips 9, 10, 11 and 12 on all four blocks, rotating in the correct sequence.

FOURTH ROUND
Measure and cut the fourth round as follows:

▌In light values –
Strip 13 – 1½ in × 7½ in (4 cm × 19 cm)
Strip 14 – 1½ in × 8 in (4 cm × 20.5 cm)
▌In dark values –
Strip 15 – 1½ in × 8½ in (4 cm × 22 cm)
   Strip 16 – 1½ in × 9 in (4 cm × 23 cm).

Place strip 13 right side down against strip 9 so you have three raw edges together. Tack (baste) and turn the block over. Now stitch just inside the previous row of stitching on the back of the block, to ensure that the stitching on round 3 does not show on the front of the block. Turn back over, remove the tacking and fold the strip over to reveal the right side of the fabric; press this flat against the backing.

Repeat this process with strips 14, 15 and 16, rotating the block and pressing each strip flat as you work. Repeat on the other three blocks.

The fourth round is now complete. Measure ¾ in (19 mm) from the last seam and draw a line around the outside of the block on the front. Stitch along this line with a straight stitch to fasten the final round of strips to the backing, and trim away excess fabric close to this line of stitching. This gives a ¼ in (6 mm) seam allowance round each block for joining the blocks together.

JOINING THE BLOCKS
Refer to the picture and arrange the blocks in order. Join them in sets of four, and

join these in sets of four again. Join these up to make the two halves of the quilt.

Finally, stitch one long seam across the middle. Press all the seams open as you go. Turn ¼ in (6 mm) in all around the outside of the quilt, tack it down and press.

BACKING THE QUILT AND FINISHING

This type of log cabin quilt does not need any wadding (batting) as the base squares form the filler. Smooth the 64 in (155 cm) square cotton backing over the back of the quilt, then pin and tack the layers together. Trim the backing to ½ in (13 mm) around the edge and turn this raw edge inside so that the edges of the quilt top and backing are even. Tack (baste) the two layers together round the edge and remove the previous tacking. Stitch the quilt top to the backing by sewing machine, stitching in the 'ditch' of the seams between the blocks. Start with the centre seams and work outwards. Use either a neutral-coloured thread that will blend in with all the colours, or an invisible filament, with thread to match the backing in the bobbin.

Finally, slip hem the quilt top to the back by hand all around the outside edge of the quilt.

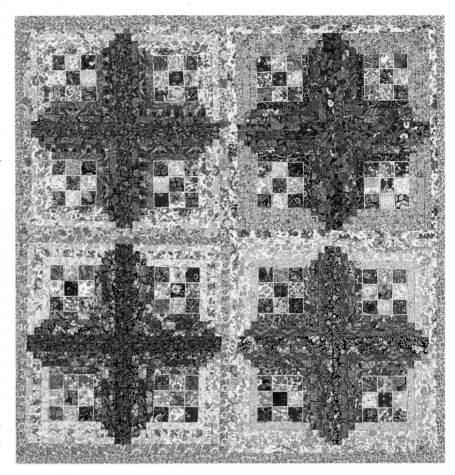